Accelerated Learning

Discover How High Performers Learn New Skills Fast, Improve Memory, Develop Laser-Sharp Focus, and Increase Their Productivity Using Techniques Such as Speed Reading

© **Copyright 2020**

All Rights Reserved. No part of this audiobook may be reproduced in any form without permission in writing from the author. Reviewers may quote brief passages in reviews.

Disclaimer: No part of this publication may be reproduced or transmitted in any form or by any means, mechanical or electronic, including photocopying or recording, or by any information storage and retrieval system, or transmitted by email without permission in writing from the publisher.

While all attempts have been made to verify the information provided in this publication, neither the author nor the publisher assumes any responsibility for errors, omissions or contrary interpretations of the subject matter herein.

This audiobook is for entertainment purposes only. The views expressed are those of the author alone, and should not be taken as expert instruction or commands. The reader is responsible for his or her own actions.

Adherence to all applicable laws and regulations, including international, federal, state and local laws governing professional licensing, business practices, advertising and all other aspects of doing business in the US, Canada, UK or any other jurisdiction is the sole responsibility of the purchaser or reader.

Neither the author nor the publisher assumes any responsibility or liability whatsoever on the behalf of the purchaser or reader of these materials. Any perceived slight of any individual or organization is purely unintentional.

Contents

INTRODUCTION 1
CHAPTER 1: ACCELERATED LEARNING 3
   HERE IS THE BRIEF HISTORY OF ACCELERATED LEARNING 3
   SO, WHAT EXACTLY IS ACCELERATED LEARNING? 4
   ACCELERATED LEARNING ALSO HAS OTHER PRINCIPLES IT ADHERES TO 5
   WHAT MAKES ACCELERATED LEARNING SPECIAL AND EFFECTIVE? 5
CHAPTER 2: WHY DO YOU NEED ACCELERATED LEARNING? 7
CHAPTER 3: HOW TO GET STARTED WITH ACCELERATED LEARNING 11
   HOW CAN YOU NURTURE THE RIGHT MINDSET TOWARD ACCELERATED LEARNING? 11
   ACCELERATED LEARNING GOAL SETTING 11
   WHY IS IT IMPORTANT TO SET GOALS TOWARD MASTERING ACCELERATED LEARNING? 12
   HOW SHOULD YOU SET GOALS TOWARD ACCELERATED LEARNING? 14
CHAPTER 4: SUPER-FAST WAYS TO LEARN NEW SKILLS 21
   ACCELERATED LEARNING TECHNIQUES THAT WILL HELP YOU LEARN ANY SKILL FAST 24
   WHAT IS SPEED READING? 30
   TIM FERRISS SPEED READING TECHNIQUE 32
   HOW DOES IT WORK? 32
   METHOD 1: TRACKERS AND PACERS 35

Method 2: Perceptual Expansion 36

Other Speed-Reading Techniques 38

CHAPTER 5: THE PRODUCTIVE PRO: 5 ELON MUSK TECHNIQUES 42

A BRIEF HISTORY OF ELON MUSK 44

CHAPTER 6: MNEMONICS: TOP 10 MEMORY RETENTION TRICKS.55

How Your Brain Recalls Memory 56

Encoding 56

Storing 57

Retrieving 58

What Are Mnemonic Techniques? 59

CHAPTER 7: MAXIMIZE YOUR FOCUS: 12 WAYS TO FOCUS MORE EFFECTIVELY 67

How Do You Concentrate? 68

CHAPTER 8: MASTERING INTENTION AND THE SUCCESS MINDSET........... 78

Mastering Intention 78

What Is Intentional Thinking? 79

How Does Intentional Thinking Impact Learning? 79

How Can You Be Intentional in Your Thinking? 82

SUCCESS MINDSET 83

So How Can You Cultivate a Success Mindset When Setting an Intention? 84

CHAPTER 9: HIGH PERFORMER BRAIN HACKS 87

Tony Robbins 87

Gary Vaynerchuk 93

Grant Cardone 95

CHAPTER 10: OBSTACLES TO LEARNING AND COMMON MISTAKES 98

Common Mistakes and How to Fix Them 104

CHAPTER 11: BONUS: THE ACCELERATED LEARNING PLAN WORKSHEET 107

How Do You Create a Learning Plan? 107

CONCLUSION 111

Introduction

In 1907, a psychologist named William James wrote an article that argued that humans only use a small part of their mental capacity. How many times have you worked on something that required so much brain energy that you went home thinking to yourself, "I must have exhausted everything I have in my brain." It is a common scenario, but the truth remains, you only used a small amount of your brain's potential that day.

How can you explain the amount of brain usage of a person like Teddy Roosevelt, who was able to read two-to-three books per day and recite a whole newspaper like it was right in front of him? How can you explain the amount of brain power that Kim Peek used to be able to memorize every word of every book he ever picked up and read? And last but not least, how does the world have over 30 people who have super memory retention abilities that help them pull events that occurred on a specific date from their memories—like telling you exactly what they ate for breakfast, lunch, and dinner, on July 23, 1992?

All these cases have greater use of the brain's potential written all over them.

The question is; how can you do that? Simple—by leveraging the power of accelerated learning.

Accelerated learning is the most advanced learning and teaching method that is in use today. A lot of the leading educational institutions and organizations have today turned to accelerated learning as their mode of teaching, which is not a surprise, considering how good the method is at improving focus, productivity, and memory. In fact, it is said to have the ability to improve your memory by up to 50%.

The thing about accelerated learning is that it naturally pushes you to use a bigger part of your brain's resources when dealing with your day to day life activities.

And if you wish to achieve all that and much more, this audiobook is going to introduce you to this amazing learning technique.

By reading this audiobook, you will get to learn what accelerated learning or "AL" is, what its tricks and techniques are and how you can use them to learn new skills fast, improve memory, develop laser-sharp focus and increase your productivity.

So, if you are here and your goal is to:

> 1. Acquire skills that will enable you to learn faster in school or at work.
>
> 2. Elevate your self-learning ability for your own self-development purposes.
>
> 3. Improve your productivity, focus, and memory, which are getting weak due to age.

Then this guide is for you.

Let's get into it starting with an introduction to accelerated learning.

I hope you enjoy it!

Chapter 1: Accelerated Learning

As a newbie in accelerated learning, the first thing you must learn about is the history of accelerated learning. This is important because it will lay some foundation that will help you understand what AL is and what it advocates for.

Here Is the Brief History of Accelerated Learning

Accelerated Learning was started in early 1960 and just like many discoveries, it wasn't known as "accelerated learning" in the beginning.

Let's take it from the top.

In the early 1960s, a Bulgarian professor and psychotherapist called Dr. Georgi Lozanov from Sofia, Bulgaria found an interest in cases of "extraordinary" people. "Extraordinary" people in this case were people who were able to use a high percentage of their brain's capacity.

He was so amused by them that he decided to do a study with them in mind—but with the aim of finding out how he could improve his teaching as a language teacher. However, the knowledge he ended up gaining after the study was nothing like he expected, so instead of him just using it to better his teaching, he decided to develop it into a new teaching style called "Suggestology."

The Suggestology model of teaching was created to make learning a natural and pleasurable process. It did that by combining actual learning with the use of games, role-playing, art, and music. At the heart of the Suggestology learning approach was Dr. Lozanov's huge emphasis on the learning environment and the teacher's attitude. He believed that a teacher should create and maintain a good learning space, which is emotionally safe and has the ability to motivate the learner to explore their full potential.

Dr. Lozanov believed this method would have a huge impact on his students; and he was right. He tested it on 416 students, and they ended up learning 80 foreign words in one hour; a period they would normally use to learn 7 foreign words. The teaching model was later renamed, in the 1970s, into what we know today as "accelerated learning" in the U.S.

Over the years, a number of professionals, researchers, and academics, have engaged in various aspects of the educational training program (accelerated learning or AL) and have developed and increased the idea of AL. Today it is mostly used in corporate training, where it's considered to be a time and cost saving training program.

So, What Exactly Is Accelerated Learning?

Accelerated learning can be defined as a multidimensional approach to learning that creates an environment where you as a student can absorb and hold on to information in a multisensory and natural way.

Let me break it down for you.

Accelerated learning is based on one simple principle, *"knowledge is not something you are supposed to absorb but something you need to create."*

What this means is that AL is an activity based and learner driven method. In an accelerated learning class, you are not engaged in short exercises that make you follow the instructor's presentations; you are instead encouraged to discover and create your own knowledge through authentic experiences and activities, which enable you to acquire greater learning.

In AL, the teacher is only supposed to deliver content to supplement your process of discovery and creation as a learner.

Let's assume that for one minute you are learning about a flower. An accelerated learning class will provide you with facts about flowers, but learning won't end there; you will be required to visit a garden, find a flower, smell the flower and feel its parts as you learn their names. You will also need to observe the flower and how it functions to get a chance to create knowledge for yourself.

It doesn't stop there though ...

Accelerated Learning Also Has Other Principles It Adheres To

The ideas behind accelerated learning are so rich that it is hard to come up with a small number of core principles. That said, there are four principles, which are seen as central.

The principles include:

- We humans have multiple senses and the more you engage them, the better you will learn.

- When you create resources, you build energy and that is more efficient than consuming content when it comes to learning.

- The more variety you get as a learner, the better you learn.

- You learn best when in an inspiring, accommodating and relaxed environment.

What Makes Accelerated Learning Special and Effective?

Accelerated learning is special because it is founded on the way we humans have evolved to learn best. The method taps into the brain's potential that has been left untouched by the conventional learning methods for so long, which is the potential that comes from you using your senses when learning.

AL involves using the whole of you as part of the learning process, and this is through the use of color, images, music, creativity, and physical activities, among other methods that help you get deeply involved in your own learning process.

But why is it important for the whole of you to get involved in a learning process?

The reason why it's important is because the human brain is not a sequential processor that understands information better when in a particular serial order. Instead, it is a parallel processor and a parallel processor blossoms when it is fully engaged in doing different activities at once.

In short, you as a human learn best when you are exposed to a rich variety of learning options.

Chapter 2: Why Do You Need Accelerated Learning?

Here are a few points that will show you why you need accelerated learning—or why it is important for you.

1. It speeds up your learning process.

Do you admire geniuses? Your answer is probably: "Yes." One of the reasons why you are fascinated with geniuses is because of their ability to learn things fast.

But is fast learning only reserved for geniuses? The answer is: "No." With accelerated learning, you too can learn faster and speed up your learning process.

Accelerated learning provides you with skills that help you to master—through habit—the ability to process fresh information in a short amount of time. It also helps you to understand new concepts faster and gives you the capacity to quickly expand your abilities and knowledge.

Some of the techniques that accelerated learning uses to speed up your learning ability include: teaching you how to break up huge information into tiny chunks so that you can learn faster, and teaching you how to turn a learning process into a game with rules and rewards.

2. It saves you time and money.

In the 19th century, our forefathers had a very different learning system. Their learning system provided them with the knowledge they needed to survive their whole career.

For example, a man who studied carpentry was taught everything he needed to know to do carpentry for the rest of his working life. Today, that luxury of taking a course once and using that knowledge to work throughout your career is no longer there—and this is mainly because of technology.

The world today changes fast, and for you to keep up with it, you will need to constantly learn new things. Accelerated learning will save you time and money in this process.

For instance, if you are a worker, your time is always limited, which means it is almost impossible for you to take a refresher course. That's where accelerated learning comes in.

With accelerated learning, you have access to highly-rated, fast learning techniques that will help you to understand what you are supposed to know—in half the time it would have taken you in normal circumstances.

3. It improves your social life.

One of the features of accelerated learning is its emphasis on working together, which helps a lot when it comes to the improvement of your social life.

With A.L, the assumption is that all participants are learning the same thing, which essentially means there will be times when you all have to work together.

This is mainly so because learners tend to understand a subject more when they interact with different students who have different views and different ways of understanding various topics.

Apart from improving your understanding, learning together also benefits you by improving your social life, especially if you are a "geek" or a busy worker who spends most of your time without much social interaction.

In an AL class, you get to talk to other people and share ideas. That process is what makes you realize you share common interests with your classmates and that more often than not blossoms into friendships and new socializing opportunities.

4. It's a holistic learning process.

The conventional learning process is mostly focused on the results you get at the end of a course. Unfortunately, this encourages you to be a "memorizing machine" that memorizes answers in order to pass exams.

What is wrong with that approach, you may ask?

The bad thing about this type of learning is that you go home without developing any new skills.

AL is different because it offers you a holistic learning system. It does this by teaching you how to internalize the information you learn and how to go to the next level, which is the application of that information into real life situations.

For example, when you are taught how to be a marketer in A.L, you are not only provided with the theory part of being a marketer but the practical part too.

Let me give you an example:

Let's assume the topic that you are learning right now is about how you can sell a product or an idea to a client.

In accelerated learning, you will be required to visit a real company and pitch them one of your ideas. The other alternative is that you can engage in a game that will provide you with a platform to apply the knowledge you have just learned.

Whatever the method, the bottom line is that you will come out of that experience with a holistic—or complete—understanding of a topic, which is more than you can say for the conventional way of learning.

Amazing, right? You are probably speechless; but yes, you have just witnessed one of the best learning systems available, in action.

I mean, how many people can boast of ever going through a learning system that makes them get fast and better results by allowing them to learn in a way that humans were designed to learn?

The question in your mind right now must be; "How can I adopt the accelerated learning system and use it to learn new skills fast, develop sharp focus, improve memory and increase my productivity as an undergraduate or postgraduate student?"

The answer to that is simple: you need to follow a step-by-step process that will equip you with tricks and techniques that will enable you to become the person that you desire to be—i.e. someone who has:

- A good memory retention ability.

A sharp focus.

- An increased level of productivity.
- An ability to learn new skills fast.

The first step in the process of you developing accelerated learning skills and qualities is you learning how to set goals toward accelerated learning—and that is what you are going to learn in the next chapter.

Chapter 3: How to Get Started with Accelerated Learning

Here is a little secret; the success of anything that you do in life is highly dependent on the mindset that you have toward what you are doing. If your mindset is wrong, you will fail. But if it is right, you will succeed.

The process of mastering accelerated learning is not an exception to this rule. You will need to create the right mindset toward AL for you to succeed at it.

How Can You Nurture the Right Mindset Toward Accelerated Learning?

There are two different ways to build the right mindset toward accelerating your learning:

1. Creating goals.
2. Creating checklists.

Let's discuss each of these in depth.

Accelerated Learning Goal Setting

For you to have a positive mindset—or any kind of mindset for that matter—you need to have a goal.

Goal setting is not a new concept though. We've all asked ourselves questions meant to shape how we live our lives. For instance:

- Why am I in this world?

- What is my purpose?
- What is my ideal job?
- What do I want to achieve in my job and how will a successful outcome look or even feel for me?

If you've asked yourself these questions, they probably helped you rediscover yourself and further enabled you to come up with goal statements to guide you through life.

A goal statement might sound like this:

"My purpose in life is to be a good cook. I will enroll myself in a cooking school and study for three years, find work after I graduate, work for a period of four years and then open up my own restaurant."

The accelerated learning process is no different to other goals; it also needs you to plan for it if you are ever to be successful in it. In other words, it needs you to set goals toward it.

So, what is a goal?

A goal can be described as a desired result or a future idea that you dream of, plan toward, and commit yourself to achieve. In short, any plan that you have about your future is your goal, and this is regardless of the type of plan you have. It can be you planning to watch a movie next weekend or you planning to clean your house tomorrow.

Why Is It Important to Set Goals Toward Mastering Accelerated Learning?

Here are some of the reasons why setting goals in AL is important.

1. Having goals gives you focus.

One of the most watched sports in the world today is soccer. Now imagine watching a soccer game that had no goal posts. That game would be pointless because it doesn't have a target. The players could have talent, great ball possession, and ability, but all that would be useless because there would be no purpose; i.e. without a goal post where the players can score, it's just men randomly kicking a ball around a field. This is exactly how life is when you don't have a goal.

When you set a goal toward A.L, you create a target that you can aim at using your effort. For instance, when you say, "I am going to read two books in a month," that goal gives your reading efforts a purpose and that automatically increases your focus.

2. Goals motivate you.

Did you know that everything that has ever motivated you in this life is deeply rooted in a goal? Why were you motivated to work hard in school? The answer is so that you could pass your exams. Why are you motivated to work hard at your job? The probable answer is for you to make enough money to cater for your needs, whatever they may be. Do you get the idea?

So, when you set goals in your accelerated learning journey, what you are doing is creating a foundation for your drive. In short, you build up some motivation that makes you want to do the work to achieve an aim you are excited about.

3. Goals break down your impossible-looking mountains into walk-able hills.

The other advantage of setting up goals is that good goals have the ability to break down huge and impossible-looking goals into smaller, doable goals.

Your reason for going through the process of accelerated learning—wanting to increase your productivity, focus, and your memory, is not a small task.

So, when you set a goal, you get the opportunity to make your life easier because you can break that huge end-goal into chewable bite sized goals.

4. Goals enable you to measure your progress.

Another advantage of setting a goal in accelerated learning is being able to measure your progress. A goal helps you gauge where you are in regard to your aim. For instance, if you aim to read a 400-page book in 40 days, it is easier for you to track your progress because you know that after every ten days, you will need to have read 100 pages.

Indeed, goal setting is an important component of success. Unfortunately, many of us don't achieve the goals we set, including our New Year's resolutions! We get side-tracked by the many distractions all around us. But why do you think that is so?

Well, the reason why you don't achieve some of your goals is simply because they are never compelling enough for you to work on, without being distracted. As you set out on a journey to master accelerated learning, you should make sure your goals are compelling enough to jolt you into action.

The question is ...

How Should You Set Goals Toward Accelerated Learning?

The best way to set a goal toward accelerated learning is to set an inspiring goal. These are goals that excite you and make you want to jump out of your bed and put time and energy into accomplishing them.

Here is a step-by-step method of how you can set your accelerated learning goals in a way that jolts you into action.

Step 1: Question yourself.

The first step to setting an exciting goal in AL is asking yourself two very important questions:

1. What is your goal?

The first question you must ask yourself is: *"What do I really want to achieve through the accelerated learning process?"*

- Do you want to improve your memory?
- Do you desire to learn new skills fast?
- Do you want to have a laser sharp focus?
- Do you want to increase your productivity?
- Or do you want to achieve all of the above?

Be very specific on what improved memory means (something measurable is best, for example: being able to remember 60 numbers from a list of 100 after reading them for ten minutes.)

Don't stop there; be specific on what learning new skills fast; having laser sharp focus; and increased productivity means to you (something you can measure).

2. What is your purpose?

The second question you need to ask yourself is: *"Why do I want to achieve that goal that I have? What will achieving that goal bring me?"*

- Will improving your memory and developing a sharp focus help you to pass exams for the remainder of your learning years?

- Will enhancing your focus increase your productivity at work and earn you that promotion you badly need?

- Will learning new skills fast help you to adapt to your ever-evolving work environment?

These two questions help you to figure out what you really want from the process of accelerating your learning.

Step 2: Figure out which type of goal you have.

The next step is you figuring out what type of goal you have.

What do I mean by this?

Ask yourself; "What is the timeline of my goal?" Is your goal a short-term goal, long-term goal or a lifelong goal? I know you are wondering how they are all different ...

Here is the difference:

- **A long-term goal.** This is a goal that takes a long period of time to achieve. It might take you a number of months or years. Improving your focus and memory to perform well or to be at the top of your class for the rest of your school years is an example of a long-term goal.

- **A short-term goal.** This is a goal that takes less than a year to achieve. Enhancing your focus to earn a promotion at work is an example of a short-term goal.

- **A lifelong goal.** This is a goal that can take a lifetime to accomplish. A good example is saying that you want to increase your productivity, in order to have saved at least $2 million by the time you retire at 60 years old.

Step 3: Create a goal using the SMART goal setting formula.

The third and last step to setting an exciting goal is finding a good technique that can help you set a compelling goal.

The truth is that there might be a couple of good ones out there, but none of them measures up to the efficiency of the S.M.A.R.T goal method, which is what you are going to use here.

The SMART goal setting method has one general principle; i.e. for your goal to be effective, it needs to be "SMART" (the abbreviation for *Specific, Measurable, Achievable, Realistic, and Time bound.*)

Here is what each word in the abbreviation entails:

Specific. Your goal needs to be detailed. In other words, make your goal as specific as you can. For instance, instead of you saying you want to pass your end of semester exam, you can say you want to get an "A" in your exam, which is more detailed.

Measurable. Your goal needs to have some clear milestones that you can use to measure your progress toward your goal. For instance, wanting to be a good real estate agent is not a measurable goal, because it doesn't define "good." A measurable goal is saying you want to be: "A real estate agent that makes four sales in a month."

Achievable. Your goal also needs to be attainable. What this means is that you cannot say you want to be the best dancer by next week, as that doesn't happen overnight. When setting a goal, you should think and see if you have the tools, resources, and skills to achieve it. If you don't, then you must learn how to acquire those skills, resources, and tools first.

Realistic. Your goal needs to be relevant. We can all dream big in our goals but what we shouldn't do is set unrealistic goals, like saying we want to start the biggest restaurant in the country if we clearly don't have the capacity to do so, or if we say we want to open a liquor store in a predominantly Christian neighborhood where alcohol is frowned upon.

Time bound. For your goal to be successful, it needs to have a target date for deliverables or milestones. This is very important. After specifying your goal, you need to set goal deadlines. This will create a sense of urgency, which will also serve as motivation for you to get going.

To get back to our topic of setting SMART goals pertaining to accelerated learning, let's discuss how to use the SMART formula to pass a French language exam. For example:

> **1. Specific.** "I failed my last French exam and got a D minus. I want to improve my performance by working on my ability to learn the new language fast. I also want to work on my focus and my memory power. I want to achieve a B grade in my next exam."
>
> **2. Measurable.** "In my first month of learning French, I should be able to read French and understand what I am reading. In my second month, I should be able to write a two-to-three paragraph story in French and in the next two months, I should be able to sing, talk, and punctuate in French."
>
> **3. Achievable.** "Improving my focus, memory, and learning skills will need work so I will set aside three hours every day to study French. I will watch French tutorials, join a French study group and engage in French learning games to get a better understanding of the language."
>
> **4. Realistic.** "My main aim is to use a multidimensional approach to learning and improving my French."
>
> **5. Time-bound.** "In four months, I should be proficient in the French language. My writing, reading, and understanding of the language should have improved and I will be in a position to pass my exams."

Now you know how to create a compelling goal that sets the right mindset toward the accelerated learning process. Next, we will discuss checklists.

Accelerated Learning Checklists

It's now time to look at the checklist component that will help you to nurture a positive mindset toward accelerated learning.

What is a checklist?

Well, a checklist can be defined as a type of list that is meant to make your work easier, by documenting tasks that you may not remember. A good example of a checklist is a "work schedule" or a "to-do" list.

As you work toward accelerated learning, a checklist is important for you because of the following reasons:

- ✓ **It helps with consistency.**

A checklist literally keeps you in check, by telling you exactly what you need to do. For instance, when your checklist indicates you need to read a book when you have free time, that statement serves as a constant reminder to you. This enables you to be consistent with whatever you want to do, which in this case is reading as much as you can (something that comes in handy in helping you accelerate your learning).

- ✓ **It helps lift some burden from your brain.**

Checklists normally act as your memory. A checklist acts as the custodian of records that you would have otherwise needed to keep in your brain.

What this does is free your brain from a memory workload. This burden relief for your brain gives it more free space, which it uses to intensify your sharpness and focus, which helps in the process of accelerating learning.

- ✓ **It helps reduce errors.**

"To err is human ..." That is one of the most popular sayings around and it is actually true. We are all prone to make an error or a mistake in life. The advantage of a checklist is that it reduces your chances of making that mistake. It does that by laying out for you what needs to be done so that you don't miss out on anything.

Here is an accelerated learning checklist inspired by Elon Musk:

- ☐ I stand my ground even if I come out as odd.

- ☐ I binge on things I am interested in.
- ☐ I can do anything that makes sense to the process of accelerating my learning.
- ☐ I can reach out for help when stuck.
- ☐ I can sacrifice to get what I want.
- ☐ I am a go-getter.
- ☐ I am willing to try different formulas to get it right.
- ☐ I can pursue any journey that leads to my dream, even if it scares me.
- ☐ I can take a risk.
- ☐ I can partner with a like-minded individual.
- ☐ I don't believe in failing.
- ☐ I only care about results.
- ☐ I invest all my efforts in what I am interested in.
- ☐ I can put a pause on anything I am doing just to pursue a project I like.
- ☐ I am not afraid to be ridiculed if that is what it means to do what I love.
- ☐ I pursue side projects as often as possible.

One big question now is; where are you at this moment in regard to being ready for accelerated learning?

To know that, please take five minutes to think about the points you have just read and check those that are true to you at this moment.

For instance, if you are a risk taker, you can go ahead and check the point that said "I can take a risk."

How many points have you checked? Are they five, ten, or maybe sixteen out of sixteen? Whatever your answer is, it can be placed in either of two categories.

1. **Ten or more points checked**. If you have checked ten points and above, it means you belong to this category. Being in this category means you are experienced and disciplined enough to jump into accelerated learning. In short, you are qualified to go to the next step.

2. **Less than ten points checked.** If you have checked nine points or less then this is your category. If you are in this category, it means you need to develop more skills for you to be ready to jump into accelerated learning. That said, you don't need to panic because this guide will come in handy in helping you develop the skills you need to be excellent at accelerating your learning.

Now that you know how to write your goal and come up with a checklist, you are ready to discover how to learn new skills fast, improve memory, develop laser-sharp focus, and increase your productivity using accelerated learning: one step at a time.

Chapter 4: Super-Fast Ways to Learn New Skills

We are all learning beings—this can be seen straight from the earliest humans, who depended on learning to have a better chance of survival. They learned how to make better tools for hunting and how to come up with efficient ways of hunting.

Fast forward to today and nothing has really changed. You can be a student, a worker, or a retired person, but learning will still be an integral part of your life. In fact, by reading this book, you are either learning something new or planning to learn something in the future.

Here is a funny thing though; despite us spending thousands of hours learning, many of us are still unable to use our learning capabilities to their full potential. This is especially true because we use learning methods that are very slow, something that makes learning harder than it has to be.

The good news is that through accelerated learning, you will learn techniques and tricks that can help you master things faster than you have all your life. The AL techniques are so powerful they could make you look like a genius when it comes to grasping new information, and the good thing about them is that you can apply them in any area of your life—in school, at work, in a seminar, or literally any other aspect of your life.

So, what are these techniques and how do they work?

First, it is vital for you to know why it is important for you to learn new things, and why you should strive to do so often.

Benefits of learning something new.

If you keenly follow extremely successful people, you've probably heard a thing or two about them emphasizing the need to read a lot. But why do you have to read a lot anyway?

Here are some reasons:

1. You get an improved memory.

Any runner out there will tell you that all it takes for them to run a long distance within a short period of time is them training their body to do so.

Your mind, just like your body, can be trained to be more efficient than it already is—and that's where learning something new comes in.

Learning something new usually trains your mind to be sharp, which automatically improves your memory.

Here is how:

When you learn new things, your mind stays active. That process of brain activation flexes your memory muscles, something that improves your brain's memory capabilities. It makes you better at remembering things and remembering them fast. But that's not all; when you decide to share the new thing that you have learnt, what normally happens is your memory gets improved even further.

2. Your brain chemistry is rewired.

Learning something new does not just give you knowledge; it also does something to your brain that makes you learn much better and faster.

So, what exactly does it do to your brain?

Learning something new increases the density of myelin in your brain. Myelin insulates nerve fibers and makes up the white matter that is found in your brain. The function of myelin is to improve your performance on a couple of tasks. When you learn something new or practice a new skill, myelin density is increased and as you saw above, that translates into you learning better and faster.

3. It increases your speed of learning.

When you learn new things over a long period of time, what normally happens is you gradually increase your speed of learning. How?

A lot of skills and information that you learn are interconnected. This information builds off each other, which make it easier for you to learn the next set of new things and learn them fast.

For instance, if you learn how to build a two story building from scratch and then after a few months, you are required to build an eight story building, learning how to make the eight story building will be easier and faster for you because you already know how to build a two story one.

4. It helps you fight off dementia.

Dementia is a group of conditions/diseases that cause impairment in some of the brain's functions, such as judgment and memory. It (dementia) is usually linked to demyelination of your brain, which can affect anyone.

But here is something interesting; when you learn new skills, your chances of having dementia become reduced. This is because when you learn new information or skills, you keep your brain active, which not only makes your neural pathways ready for new impulses to pass along but also denies your brain the chance to demyelinate. These two factors are what make it harder for you to develop dementia.

5. It makes you a more interesting person.

Learning new information usually turns you into a well-rounded person—a person who is knowledgeable in different areas of life; like sports, entertainment, business, or politics.

The benefit of this is that you become very relatable to other people. You can easily meet a stranger and connect with them immediately, because you are well versed in most topics and interests. Being an interesting person also improves the quality of your life. This is because you can draw people toward you and form strong and meaningful friendships.

Experts say the same way physical exercises keep your body fit, learning new skills and information helps to keep your mind fit. When your mind is fit, your brain becomes sharp and makes it easier for you to learn fast. This goes on to show you just how important it is for you to learn new things.

Now back to the big question: what techniques can help you to learn new information fast and how do they work?

Accelerated Learning Techniques That Will Help You Learn Any Skill Fast

Here is a list of the accelerated learning techniques and tricks that can help you learn new skills super-fast.

Technique 1: Deconstruct a skill into small pieces.

Deconstructing a skill into small pieces is an amazing technique that can help you to consume information much faster.

Your conventional way of learning has unknowingly conditioned you to take too much time to learn new skills or acquire new information.

How has it done that?

It has done that by making you look at any skill you are about to learn as one big task.

Why is this wrong?

When a task looks big and challenging to you, what normally happens is you start looking for distractions because you really don't know where to start. This is why sometimes when you want to learn a new language, instrument—or just about anything else—you find yourself browsing the internet, talking to a friend or doing anything other than what you are supposed to do within the first few hours.

So, what is the solution?

The solution and the first technique that you can use to learn faster is to deconstruct the skill you are about to learn into small pieces or milestones that you can focus on doing, as you build up toward mastering the actual skill.

Take learning to be a driver, for example. If you say you are going to get into a car and start figuring out how to drive, you may have a very bad experience and it might take you months to actually learn how to drive.

But if you break down learning how to drive a car into smaller lessons, your learning curve is accelerated and you can take less time to master the art of driving.

In your case of wanting to learn how to drive a car, you can break it down into four tasks.

Task 1: Familiarize yourself with the pedals and know how to handle the gears.

Task 2: Understand the basic dashboard controls.

Task 3: Learn how to drive a car and how to reverse the car.

Task 4: Learn advanced driving techniques, like parking.

In simple terms, breaking up your goal into bite sized tasks helps your brain to stop jumping up and down trying to find where to start and where to go next. It instead gives your brain direction and purpose. Your brain gets a clear message of what it needs to focus on at any given time; where that task ends; and where to go from there.

Technique 2: Implement the 80/20 rule.

The 80/20 rule, or the Pareto principle—as it is most commonly known—is one of the best strategies that you can use to speed up your learning.

An economist named Vilfredo Pareto developed the 80/20 rule in the year 1906. What the rule states is *"80% of the results you get come from 20% of your input."* Over the years, this rule has been proven to be true in relationships, business, learning, and in every other facet of human life.

But how does it speed up your learning?

To apply the 80/20 rule in accelerated learning, you need to identify the few most effective strategies that bring the most progress and focus on them.

Let me break it down for you:

If 20% of your friends influence you positively 80% of the time, this means that the other 80% of your friends influence you positively only 20% of the time!

What the 80/20 rule tells you to do is to look for the 20% of your friends who add value to you and concentrate on them alone. That way, you will get 80% of their positive influence and not waste time with the majority of people that bring very little positive influence.

When it comes to learning a new course or a new skill, you can apply the 80/20 rule and learn faster, by using it to identify the studying style that is most effective for you.

Therefore, instead of using four study techniques that take you eight hours a day to study, you can look deep within you and figure out which studying style is most effective for you.

Is it:

- ✓ Being taught by a teacher?
- ✓ Watching tutorials on YouTube?
- ✓ Having a study group?
- ✓ You reading on your own?

Find the most effective method and stick with it. This will save you time.

In language, you can use the 80/20 rule to learn faster by learning the top 100 most common words that you know make up approximately 50% of the total written content in all languages. This will help you to understand most spoken and written words in any language that you take on.

Technique 3: Use the Pomodoro technique.

As a learner, you know too well how distracting a learning process can be, especially in today's world where we have our phones, tablets and even our laptops next to us when we are learning.

For instance, have you ever done a task and halfway through, you have found yourself watching a video on YouTube that is unrelated to the task at hand? Or you are checking your email while keeping an eye on your Facebook page? We have all experienced procrastination of some kind.

Well, distractions are one of the major reasons why you end up learning in the slowest way possible because they take up a lot of your time.

What is the solution?

Simple: try the Pomodoro technique.

The Pomodoro technique is a time management method that has a very simple concept, which is: *for you to be as productive as you can possibly be, you need to work or learn for 25 minutes and then take a five-minute break.*

In short, it stipulates that you divide your learning time into 30-minute blocks. In the 25 minutes of learning, the Pomodoro technique makes you focus on what you are supposed to learn at that particular moment. If your timetable says "mathematics," for example, don't use the time to study economics—no matter the temptation. In those 25 minutes, you are not supposed to check your email, check your Instagram or even multitask. It forbids you from getting distracted.

In the five minutes of break, it allows you to do anything that makes you feel relaxed. This can be checking your email, catching up with friends on Facebook, taking a walk, et cetera.

In so doing, the Pomodoro technique can help you to learn faster because it doubles—and sometimes even triples—your productivity. This is because the distractions you encounter in your conventional method of learning waste a lot of your time, with some people ending up even wasting two or more hours in a single day.

Therefore, if it took you six months to learn a new language before, with the Pomodoro technique, it can take you three months to learn the next language. That's truly a fast way of learning.

Technique 4: Teach what you have studied.

The other method that can help you to learn faster than you did before is you imagining that you are going to teach someone what you are currently learning.

According to a study done at Washington University in St. Louis, when a person imagines that they will need to teach others what they learn, it speeds up their learning and they end up remembering more than they normally do.

Why is this so?

The best way to explain this is by looking at how teachers prepare for their class. Teachers normally seek out key points in topics and then they organize that information into a logical structure. This helps them to gather lots of information within a short period of time.

That is exactly what happens to you when you pretend you are learning to teach others. You automatically turn to those types of efficient learning strategies that teachers use and that is what speeds up your learning process.

Technique 5: Use the distributed practice method.

When it comes to learning, many people prefer cramming, rather than understanding.

Sound familiar?

Unfortunately, this method of learning is slow because cramming is not learning.

For example, if you cram information in order to code, you will comfortably perform the project you are doing. But the next time you want to code, you will be forced to go back to learning how to do it, which is a huge waste of time.

The antidote of cramming and learning slowly is applying the "distributed practice method." The distributed practice method is simply a learning technique where you are made to practice what you have learned in multiple short sessions over a long period of time, with some amount of space between each session.

This is how it works:

✓ *Step 1:* Take notes when a topic is being taught in class.

✓ *Step 2:* Take one or two days off before you review the notes you took. That study session needs to take less than one hour.

✓ *Step 3:* Spread your revision sessions out to three times in a week.

In short, you are supposed to revise what you are learning in sessions of less than one hour, three times per week.

So, if you learned how to plant a tree, then one or two days later you will use one hour or less to review how to do this. After that, you will set aside three sessions in a week, which can be Monday afternoon, Wednesday morning and Friday afternoon, for example, to review how to plant a tree.

This way of studying is effective and fast because your brain usually pays more attention when you take short learning intervals. This means when you pick up a book and learn how to plant a tree on Monday, Wednesday and Friday, you will have a better understanding than the person who reads the same content once a week for three hours.

As Benedict Carey said in an interview with *The New York Times*:

"Learning is like watering a lawn. You can water your lawn once for 90 minutes but the lawn will never be as green as when you wo times in a week for 30 minutes".

Technique 6: Taking a nap.

This might come as a surprise to you—but taking a nap is one of the best techniques you can use to accelerate your learning.

The question is: how does napping accelerate learning?

A study done in the University of Lyon in France tried to investigate the impact of napping when studying. The research took 40 students and taught them Swahili translations for 16 French words, but in two sessions.

The participants were divided into two groups (the "wake" group and the "sleep" group). The wake group did their first learning session in the morning and finished with a second session in the evening—on the same day. On the other hand, the sleep group did their first learning session in the evening, went to sleep and then did the second learning session the next morning. Their recall capabilities were tested, and it emerged that the sleep group were able to recall 10 out of 16 words on average—while the wake group were only able to recall 7.5 words on average.

As you can see, taking a nap between study sessions helps you to recall more of what you have learned. In fact, new research published in *Psychological Science* states that getting sleep in between studies can boost your recall up to six months later.

When you improve your recall, what normally happens is you properly understand more things, which means it takes you less time to finish a course or even learn a new skill; like being a mechanic.

Now that you have all that information on how to train your mind to learn faster, all that is left is for you to put those techniques into action.

Think of one skill that you want to learn and use any of these six methods to learn it faster than you could have before. Feel free to combine a couple of the techniques when learning something new.

Your next step now is to learn how to speed read, as it is an important part of accelerated learning.

What Is Speed Reading?

Speed reading is a technique of reading words at an extremely fast rate—but with adequate comprehension. Speed reading usually helps you to recognize and assimilate several phrases or words at a glance, rather than you identifying individual words.

This automatically increases your reading speed. To understand the speed reading concept more, you must learn how you read in normal circumstances and how speed reading improves that.

Speed Reading: The Tim Ferriss Technique Plus More

Currently, it is almost impossible for you to retire to bed without reading something; which is understandable because reading is the all-important skill you use to access new knowledge and information.

That said, for a long time, the amount of information humans process has been gradually increasing. Twenty years ago, many of us didn't have to get information from emails, websites, and social media sites, and even those who did didn't use them as much as they do today.

Today you have books, magazines, newspapers, novels, and social media, which you read for your own pleasure. And that's not all; you also have emails, reports, and project proposals, job CV's, and educational books to read on an ongoing basis. Clearly, it's a lot—and almost everyone is feeling the pressure.

But there is some good news for you—and this is the fact that there is a method to read everything in a third or a fifth of the time. It is called speed reading.

Here is an illustration of how you tend to read and understand text normally.

When you read a book, a newspaper, or any form of text, the first thing you do is look at a word, or several words, at a glance. This is called "eye fixation" and it's the point where your eyes come to rest when you focus on words while you are reading.

After fixation, your eyes then move—or "jump"—to the next word or group of words in a movement called saccade.

Normal reading entails a cycle of you repeating fixation as well as saccades one or two times before stopping to understand the phrase you have just read. That stop takes you 0.3 – o.5 seconds on average.

That is typically how you read.

Now if you add all those fixations and saccades—along with the comprehension pauses—together, you will realize you are reading between 250-400 words per minute (WPM), which is the normal WPM rate of the average person.

Speed reading shortens the time you spend on fixation and saccades, as well as comprehension pauses, which automatically helps you to read anywhere from 500 to 1200 words per minute.

Now that you know what speed reading is, it's time for you to learn how to use it to improve your reading speed, along with your comprehension.

One of the best ways to apply speed reading is through following Tim Ferriss's speed-reading technique.

Tim Ferriss Speed Reading Technique

In 1998, a person by the name of Tim Ferriss attended a seminar dubbed "PX Project" at Princeton University. At this conference, he taught undergraduates how to improve their reading speed rate. His method was later tested, and it was proven to have an average increase in reading speed of 386%. Amazing, right?

What the undergraduates learned that day is now called the "Tim Ferriss technique."

Tim Ferriss's speed reading technique is a very simple technique that believes you can double, triple, or even quadruple your reading speed, if you follow its procedure.

So, what is its procedure?

The reading procedure is divided into three categories.

1. Introduction to the speed reading technique.

2. How to apply the speed-reading technique—.

3. Practicing reading fast but with comprehension.

How Does It Work?

This speed-reading technique can help you to improve your reading speed by making you do three things.

1. Minimize the number and duration of the fixations you have per line.

Minimizing the number and duration of your fixations is the first thing that Ferriss believes you must do to increase your reading speed.

Now you might not know this, but your eyes do not read words in a straight line.

Let's experiment and see if that is true:

Take one book, any book that is near you. Open it up and place your focus on the beginning of a page or a chapter. Use one of your fingers to close one of your eyes and use the opened eye to read the first few sentences of the book.

What have you noticed?

If you are keen, you will notice that your eye jumped from one word to another. This was because your eyes use saccadic sequence (jumping from one fixation to another) when you are reading.

And, as you now know, fixation costs you time. So, what the Tim Ferriss technique does is reduce the number of fixations, to save you time.

2. Eliminate back-skipping and regression.

Tim also believes you need to eliminate back-skipping and regression if you are to increase your reading speed.

Have you ever read a book and found yourself jumping to a line you have already read? We all do that because conscious re-reading (regression) and subconscious re-reading (back-skipping) occurs naturally to all of us.

However, these are bad habits as far as speed reading is concerned.

Why is that?

Well, for starters, these two factors usually take about 30% of your total reading time, so if you could eliminate or at least reduce them drastically, your reading speed would be completely improved.

Tim Ferriss focuses on eliminating regression and back-skipping—and that's another way his technique adds speed to your reading.

3. Introduce drills that can increase your horizontal peripheral vision span.

The other way through which the Tim Ferriss technique increases your reading speed is by taking advantage of your peripheral vision span.

Let me explain:

The way you were taught to read a book is word by word, starting from the far-left words to the far-right words. The problem with this method of reading is that you don't take advantage of your horizontal peripheral vision span.

Your peripheral vision is the part of your vision that captures everything your eye can see outside of your main area of focus. Your normal way of reading lands your peripheral vision into the blank spaces at the beginning and the end of each sentence. This makes you lose—or forego—almost 50% of your words per fixation.

The Tim Ferriss technique corrects that by teaching you how to put your peripheral vision to good use.

The question now is: how does the Tim Ferriss technique help you to minimize your fixations, eliminate regression, and improve how you use your peripheral vision? The answer is simple: by making you go through the following steps.

Step 1: Determine your WPM.

The first step in the Tim Ferriss technique is for you to calculate your word-per-minute rate, which is the words you are able to read per minute.

Why is this important?

The Tim Ferriss technique doesn't just teach you how to be a fast reader; it also measures your improvement, and to do that you must know your current reading speed.

To learn your current WPM, follow this procedure:

1. Take a book—any book you can find. Open it up and count the number of words in the first five lines. Let's assume there are 72 words.

2. Find the average number of words-per-line by dividing the number of words in the five lines by five.

   - *For example: (number of words) 72 divided by 5 (lines) = 14.4 (words per line. Round it off to 14 words per line.)*

3. Get the average number of lines per page. Count the number of total lines found on five pages and divide that number by five. Let's assume there are 164 lines on five pages.

   - *The calculation will be 164 divided by 5 = 32.8. (Round it off to get 33 lines per page.)*

4. To get the average number of words per page, multiply the number of lines per page with the number of words per line.

   - *For example: (number of lines) 33 x 14 (words per line) = 462 (words per page.)*

5. To find your accurate WPM rate, you will need to take a timer and use it to time yourself reading the book you have been looking at for one minute. Read the way you normally read, which is reading with comprehension. Remember you want to know your true words-per-minute, so don't read faster or slower than you usually do. After reading for one minute, count the lines you have read and multiply that by the average number of words per line.

Let's assume you read 19 lines. The calculation will be:

(Number of lines read) 19 x 14 (words per line) = 266 (the average words per minute.)

There you have it; your WPM, according to our example, would be 266.

Step 2: Apply the Tim Ferriss speed reading methods.

Now that you know your WPM, the next step is for you to learn and apply Tim Ferriss's speed reading techniques. Tim Ferriss uses two very powerful methods to help you accelerate your learning speed.

Let's discuss them:

Method 1: Trackers and Pacers

Trackers and pacers help you to minimize how much time you take per fixation and to eliminate back-skipping and regression.

One thing that too many fixations has in common with regression and back-skipping is that these are all caused by the lack of a visual aid, like a finger or a pen, which can help to track the words you are reading.

Your eyes read in a sequence of saccadic movements. So, when your vision is not guided, it will, at some point, start jumping all over the page. Tim Ferriss's technique for solving this is very simple; use a tracker, which will also serve as a pacer to track your reading.

In this method, you are going to use a pen. Take a pen and hold it as you would when writing. Now follow the methods below.

Technique (learn the technique first).

Open up your book where you want to read and then place your pen below the first line. Underline each line, moving from the far-left side to the far-right side of the page.

Meanwhile, your focus should be above the tip of the pen; reading as the pen underlines the line. Carry out this exercise for two minutes. As you do so, make sure the maximum time you are taking in reading one line is one second.

At this point, you should not concern yourself with comprehension. Just read and try to increase your speed with the subsequent pages.

Technique with speed (add speed to the technique).

Now draw your attention to speed. Repeat the technique of reading with your focus above the pen but this time, focus more on increasing your reading speed. You should take no more than half a second reading each line. You may not comprehend anything but that is okay and expected; this step is not meant to make you understand anything—rather, its purpose is to condition your perceptual reflexes to help you adapt to a system of speed reading. It's a speed exercise.

Carry out this technique for three minutes and try to put all your focus on the technique and speed.

Practice method one until you feel you have laid a strong foundation, and then move to the second method.

Method 2: Perceptual Expansion

As you learned earlier, much of the traditional reading style entails not taking advantage of your peripheral vision.

What you may not know is that when reading, you spend about 25-50% of your time reading margins in your peripheral field that have no content. Training your peripheral vision to be more effective can increase your reading speed by more than 300%.

That is what the second method in Tim Ferriss's technique entails—how to take advantage of your peripheral vision.

Here is how it works.

Technique 1.

Take a pen, then track, and pace your reading at a steady speed of one line per second. On the next line, begin tracking the words you are reading one word in from the first word and end one word in from the line's last word.

For instance, if the sentence you are reading is:

"Don't concern yourself with comprehension the first time you train at speed reading."

You will start tracking from "concern" and finish your tracking at "speed."

Carry out the exercise for one minute and don't concern yourself with comprehension at this point.

Technique 2.

Advance the first technique by beginning your tracking two words in from the first word of each line and end tracking two words in from the last word of the line. That said, your speed of one line per second should still remain.

Techniques with Speed Added.

Advance the technique further by starting to track the words at least three words in from the first word of each line and end your tracking three words in from the last word of the line. Repeat this technique for three minutes but take no more than half a second to read each line.

Once again, don't worry if you can't comprehend anything, as this is just an exercise that helps your system adapt to fast reading.

Practice the second method of Tim Ferriss's technique until you feel comfortable with it and then move on to the third step.

Step 3: Calculate your new WPM reading speed.

The two methods you have been practicing were meant to increase your reading speed. Now it is time for you to know how well the two methods have worked for you—and this is through you calculating your new words-per-minute rate.

Here is how to do it:

4. Set one minute on a timer and press start as soon as you start reading your first line. Read as fast as your comprehension allows.

5. Record the number of lines read. Let's assume you read 46 lines.

6. Multiply the number of lines by the average words-per-line you determined earlier to get your WPM rate.

Example: (number of lines) 46 x 14 (average words per line) = 644 (words per minute rate.)

As you will notice, your reading speed will have improved immensely. In fact, going by the above example, your WPM would have more than doubled.

This goes to show you just how great the Tim Ferriss technique is at increasing your reading speed.

Tim Ferriss's method is not the only effective speed-reading technique out there. Many other good speed-reading techniques exist that you can use to accelerate your reading speed, along with your understanding.

Other Speed-Reading Techniques

Here are a couple of these techniques:

Undo Your Bad Reading Habits

Increasing your reading speed does not always need complex techniques to be achieved. Sometimes you only need to look deep into your way of reading and try to figure out what you can change to perform better.

That is where undoing your bad reading habits comes in.

We all have some bad reading habits that could be standing in the way of us speed reading.

For instance, have you ever read a whole page in a book and didn't understand anything but when you went to the teacher, they simply told you to read again—but this time at a slower speed?

It's because your mind may have been tired, and it needed a rest.

That is one example of the bad habits you need to stop to increase your reading speed.

Here are the other bad habits that make you a slow reader and how to stop them.

> ✓ **Rereading.**

We all have found ourselves rereading text more than once—perhaps to grasp better what we have just read.

While this helps us to understand what we didn't before, most of the time it is a huge waste of our time. And I will explain three reasons why that is the case:

> ✓ You reread because you weren't paying attention when reading.
>
> ✓ You reread because the sentence didn't make any sense.
>
> ✓ You reread because the sentence was poorly written.

All of these reasons make you take more time reading than you ought to.

Now apart from the first reason, there is nothing much re-reading can do, even if you repeat it a thousand times, because the bottom line is: you won't understand the sentence.

To stop this habit, you need to stop going back to reread a sentence you didn't understand.

But how will you understand the sentence then?

Here is the trick; the next sentence you read after the one you didn't understand helps you to understand the previous one—or at least to get an idea of what it was saying.

That's not all; when you read a paragraph, you tend to get a broader meaning of the point it wanted to bring forth—regardless of whether you understood a sentence or not. This shows that you don't have to waste time rereading a line because you can get to know what it meant as you read on.

Tip: the only time you are permitted to go back and reread text is when you read a whole paragraph and you don't understand it.

✓ Reading one word at a time.

The other bad habit that makes many of us slow readers is reading one word at a time. When your focus is strictly on one word, your reading speed becomes very slow.

What you should do instead is to learn to focus your eyes on a group of words, something which increases your reading speed.

✓ Reading every text the same way.

The other bad habit that may make you a slow reader is reading everything—different types of text—using the same speed.

Why does this slow you down?

The texts that you read are different from each other. You have important texts like a textbook and emails and not-so-important texts like magazines and social media stories. For you to be fast and efficient at reading, you must learn to read at a faster rate when going through the not-so-important texts and only reduce your speed on the important ones.

✓ Lack of concentration.

Have you ever found yourself reading one sentence three-to-four times? That was caused by lack of concentration and it's one of the contributing factors to your slow reading speed.

The antidote to this is for you to try to focus more when reading and giving yourself breaks, especially when you feel your mind is tired.

✓ Get rid of sub-vocalizing.

Have you ever read a book and noticed you were mouthing along to the words? If your answer is "yes" then what you were doing was sub-vocalizing, which is what you need to get rid of to increase your reading speed.

Let me explain …

Sub-vocalizing makes you read with your talking speed because you involve your mouth in the reading process. This automatically slows you down because the fastest you can read using your talking speed is 150 words per minute.

But here is something interesting.

According to research, your brain is capable of processing up to 400 words per minute. What this means is that sub-vocalizing does not use your full potential in regard to the speed you can hit when reading.

That is why getting rid of it automatically increases your reading speed. In fact, stopping sub-vocalizing can increase the number of words you read by up to 200%.

The best way to stop sub-vocalizing is by you focusing on key words and passing over the rest of the words when reading. That said, you should make sure you understand the text you are reading.

Implementing these techniques will, without doubt, catapult your reading speed drastically, which will in turn make accelerated learning a lot easier for you.

Next, we will learn how to increase your productivity to help you make the process of accelerated learning more effective and transformative for you.

Chapter 5: The Productive Pro: 5 Elon Musk Techniques

Almost all of us wish we could get more stuff done within the 24 hours a day that we all have.

Instead of wishing, is there anything that you can possibly do to improve your productivity?

The answer is "yes" there is. In fact, you can do either of two things:

> 1. You can decide to increase your working hours. For instance, if you were to do a project for one month, you can decide to increase your daily working hours from seven hours per day to twelve hours per day and complete the project in less than one month—probably in three weeks.
>
> 2. You can decide to work smart. A good example is you finding a way to do twice as much as you would usually do in the seven hours that you work in a day. For instance, if you're a mail man and you deliver 100 letters in seven hours using a bicycle, you can buy or hire a car that enables you to deliver twice or thrice the number of letters you used to deliver in the same seven hours.

If you look at the two methods, the latter seems to be a better method of increasing productivity, as it allows you to use almost the same energy and the same hours: but to do more. As author Sam Ewing wrote, "It's not the number of hours you put in your work that counts, it's the work you put in the hours."

The question now is; how can you learn to do more in a short period of time by working smart?

It's simple; you need to look into the life of a high performer who has mastered the art of productivity and learn how they do it—and one such person that fits that criteria is Elon Musk.

Elon Musk is the perfect example of a highly productive person, which is why we will use his methods to learn how to increase productivity.

But who really is Elon Musk?

Here is a brief history of Elon Musk that shows why he is said to be arguably one of the most productive people in the world today.

A Brief History of Elon Musk

Elon Musk is an American entrepreneur and businessman who is known for founding three large corporations, namely: X.com in 1999 (it operates as PayPal today), SpaceX in 2002, as well as Tesla Motors in 2003—among doing many other things.

Elon Musk was born in 1971 in Pretoria, South Africa to a model called Maye Musk and an engineer father called Errol Musk.

Growing up, Elon Musk had a rough childhood. In school, he got bullied a lot. He didn't have a lot of friends as people thought he was weird. No one cared about a kid obsessed with electric cars and video games.

At ten years old, his parents got divorced and that's when he started developing an interest in computers. He started teaching himself basic computing and how to program. At age twelve, he developed a game called Blastar and sold it for $500.

At the age of seventeen, Musk decided to board a plane to Canada with no money and not much of a plan. Once there, he managed to convince his cousin to host him after he had said no earlier. That year, he did odd jobs, including going to the unemployment office to ask for work.

When the opportunity to enroll at Queen's University in Canada came, he grabbed it with both hands. He later transferred to the University of Pennsylvania in the US. His brother Kimbal Musk then joined him back in the US and after he graduated, the two of them went to the Bay Area and found internships.

One day, when Musk was at work, a salesman who was from a new start-up business came and tried to sell him advertising space on the internet. The pitch was awful, which made Musk think he could do better. He had never started a business before. In fact, he had no knowledge of how to start one.

Instead of going to school to learn how, he and his brother rented a studio apartment and started an online city guide called Zip2 Corporation. This was in 1995. In 1999, they sold the company to Compaq Computer Corporation for $307 million. Elon Musk walked away with $22 million, which earned him a spot in the list of multi-millionaires less than 30 years old. After the sale, Musk planned to launch his next company.

PayPal

Elon Musk and his brother combined forces to launch an online bank called X.com. Because of numerous challenges experienced with X.com, Musk decided to merge with their competitor called Confinity. Musk was the CEO, but he got removed and the company's name was changed to PayPal. He swallowed his pride and even went on to invest more in the company to become the major shareholder. He worked hard with the company until it reached elite status in business. In 2002, PayPal was sold to eBay for $1.5 billion. Elon Musk pocketed $180 million after taxes.

Just like before, Musk planned to launch his next company, and he did so by investing $100 million in a company called Space X, $70 million into a company called Tesla and $10 million into another company called Solar City.

SpaceX

Elon Musk founded his third company, Space Exploration Technologies Corporation (trading as SpaceX) in the year 2002. He invested $100 million. His intention was to build spacecraft for commercial space travel.

At first, SpaceX underwent many difficulties and at one point, it almost went bankrupt. Musk kept working and finding new investors. In 2008, his hard work paid off when SpaceX was awarded a contract to handle cargo transport for NASA's International Space Station.

In 2012, the company made history when it launched the Falcon 9 Rocket, which carried 1,000 pounds of supplies to astronauts who were in the International Space Station. Today, Elon Musk—and SpaceX in general—is working on a fleet of passengers' spaceships.

Tesla, Inc

Elon Musk is the CEO and co-founder of Tesla, Inc (originally Tesla Motors, Inc) that was founded in 2003. The company is dedicated to manufacturing affordable electric cars, solar panels and battery products. Musk is the product architect at Tesla. He also oversees all product development. Through the years, Tesla has launched powerful, fast and affordable electric cars, including the Roadster and Model S.

SolarCity

In 2006, Elon Musk helped his cousins start a solar panel company called SolarCity. In 2016, SolarCity and Tesla merged, with Musk being the majority shareholder in both entities.

So how can one person do all those things and still be CEO of more than one company?

Now you get the idea of why he is a prime example of peak productivity.

Elon Musk's story is one of hustle and persistence. He beat the odds to come from nowhere and be so successful. But what is impressive and fascinating about Elon Musk is his ability to achieve difficult things, which he often does within a ridiculously short schedule.

So, what aspects of Elon Musk's working life can you adapt in order to improve your own level of productivity?

Let's discuss some five strategies that Elon Musk uses to stay highly productive:

1. Kick start your day with the most important work.

As you now know, Elon Musk is the CEO of a good number of large corporations, including SpaceX, Tesla, and SolarCity. One of the impressive things about Elon Musk is that he always manages to stay on top of these companies on a day-to-day basis.

How does he do it?

One technique is that he starts each day with the most important tasks.

To Musk, the most critical task for him is checking and replying to his emails. Musk takes half an hour to deal with his emails and he does that to unblock other people's productivity—mostly his employees, whose work and progress halt if they don't get an approval from Musk.

So how can you apply that productive technique to your work?

You should do it by copying exactly what Musk does; find the most important task for the day and then handle it first.

Do you remember the 80/20 rule, which recommends focusing on the 20% of tasks that bring 80% of results? That's the technique you need to follow to skyrocket your productivity. Therefore, think of that one thing that you do in your job that delivers the most impact in your work.

For example, if you are an internet marketer, the most important thing for you to do is to update your social media handles.

Once you find that one MIT (most important task), build the habit of performing it before you do anything else.

That said, this technique also assists you to accelerate your learning.

How?

In everything that you learn, there are key points that—if you understand them—make the subject easier, because the rest of the information falls in between the key points.

For instance, if you are majoring in baking and pastry in school and you want to accelerate your learning, the first thing you must strive to learn is how to bake perfectly. After that, the rest of the information will be easier for you to understand, which will help you to learn faster than usual.

2. Build a foundation of wide knowledge.

If you were to analyze all CEOs of tech companies, it wouldn't be a surprise for you to find that Musk is the one CEO that understands more about the science that goes behind what his company creates, like rockets and cars.

Musk has a wide understanding in different areas, including engineering, computer science, math and physics. What is amazing is that he always tries to expand his knowledge. His brother once said that Elon Musk had a habit of reading two books a day when they were growing up.

Musk continuously learns from people who have more knowledge than him, including his employees. One such employee is Kevin Brogan, who was once questioned by Musk about his knowledge on valve and specialized materials. He thought he was being tested but later realized Musk was after the knowledge. Musk's broad knowledge helps him to understand things that his engineers explain to him, meaning he is able to interact faster with employees and get back to work on other things.

How do you apply the technique of acquiring wide knowledge to be productive?

The world today is a mixture of the older generation (born in the 60s and before that), the dot com generation—if I may call them that (born between the 70s and 90s), and the millennials (born from 2000 upwards). Those three generations are usually handled very differently.

For instance, when marketing food, you can sell easily to the older generation if the food is healthy. To the dot com generation, the food needs to be perceived as delicious, to drive huge sales. But when it comes to selling to the millennial, the food needs to be delicious *and* accessible. For instance, it should be possible to order it online. You get the point.

Acquiring broad knowledge helps you to deal with projects faster and more efficiently at work. If you were the marketer in our example, you would have easily succeeded at marketing a food product to all three generations, if you have a broad knowledge of how to deal with each.

But if you don't have the broad knowledge, you may have wasted a lot of time trying to figure out the right marketing strategy and why what you are launching is not ideal for everyone.

Gaining broad knowledge also helps you to learn faster. If you take the marketing example, broad knowledge helps you to learn how to deal with different marketing demands faster than if you weren't knowledgeable. So, it also helps you to accelerate your learning because you have a rich foundation of knowledge.

3. Set and stick to your schedule.

Not many CEOs can agree to run more than one large company—let alone three. But Elon Musk does it and he has some amazing achievements to show for it. Running more than one company is not an easy task.

One of the secret techniques that Musk uses is setting a very detailed and specific daily schedule. He breaks his calendar into five-minute windows. In those five-minute openings, he prioritizes manufacturing, design, and engineering. Eighty percent of his time entails working on these three areas.

By dividing his time into five-minute slots, Musk is able to schedule more tasks during the day.

How do you apply the scheduling technique to boost your productivity?

One of the things that stands out from Elon Musk's scheduling method is how he works from his calendar, as opposed to having a "to-do" list. This helps him to be more productive because a calendar is limited, so when he schedules a task, he gets a better sense of time because he can now determine how much time he has to complete the task.

For you to be extra productive at your work or in school, you need to do the following things:

- First—break down your days into small portions of, let's say, 30-40 minutes instead of Musk's five-minute portions. You can also find a duration that works best for you and your work type.

- Second—schedule every task you do on your calendar. For instance, if you work as a project manager, you can schedule time for talking to clients, time for meetings, time to work on your current project, time to supervise what other workers are doing, time for checking your emails, and time for lunch. Schedule all of these activities in your 30-minute slots. If you are a student, you can divide your schedule into learning by yourself, learning through practice, learning in a group study session, and learning through tutorials and listening to a teacher.

- Third—put everything on your calendar.

When you know what to do every second, you usually don't waste time. This automatically increases your productivity and enables you to learn faster.

4. Have overambitious goals.

According to Musk's critics, one of his flaws is setting overly ambitious deadlines that he can't deliver, and they are right; Tesla—led by Musk—once said it would deliver an electric car by the name Roaster in 2006 but that didn't happen. Instead, they delivered it in 2008.

What his critics did not see is that Musk had created the first electric car that was completely battery powered.

Musk sets ambitious deadlines to change people's perceptions about what is possible. This can be explained better by what one of the executives in SpaceX said about him, and I quote:

"It's like he has everyone working on this car that is meant to get fr Angeles to New York on one tank of gas. They will work on the car for and test all of its parts. Then, when they set off for New York after tho all the vice presidents think privately that the car will be lucky to ge Vegas. What ends up happening is that the car gets to New Mexico- t far as they ever expected-and Elon is still mad. He gets twice as n anyone else out of people."

How to apply the overambitious goal technique to boost your productivity.

There is a huge possibility that you have not realized your full potential at work.

To know if this is true, answer this one question:

Who is your role model in the field that you work in?

Now do you think that you are able to do what he/she does, and can you even do half of the things that he/she does? If your answer is "no," then it means you need to do much more—and the best way to do that is to set outrageous deadlines for yourself.

For instance, if you are a car sales-person and you sell two or sometimes four cars in a month, set a goal of selling twenty cars in one month. Tell your friends, colleagues, and your family about it. This adds intensity to your goal as you now have an audience watching. After that one month, you will end up having sold more cars than you used to, probably eleven cars or more.

The same concept works in accelerated learning. If you set a target of reading your engineering books for the semester by halfway through the semester, even if you don't meet your target, you will have accelerated your learning. In short, you will have outperformed your old self to be more productive.

Remember: as Parkinson's Law aptly puts it; "Work expands so as to fill the time available for its completion." If you expect more from yourself and push yourself, you will somehow find yourself delivering more!

5. Create a "growth mindset."

One of the qualities that makes Elon Musk successful in everything that he does is his "growth mindset." Musk is never satisfied with where he is. When you think he has accomplished an amazing goal, he wakes up tomorrow and reaches for a greater invention. This is because he believes that there is always an improved, faster, or cheaper way of doing things, and that this applies in every area.

In 2004, Elon Musk had a meeting with a potential SpaceX supplier. He wanted to buy an electromechanical actuator, so he asked for the cost. The supplier gave him a quote of $120,000.

Musk thought the price was too high, so he broke the components of the actuator down and told the now Director of Advanced Projects at SpaceX to build it from scratch for less than $5,000. Davis took nine months, but he finally did it and for just $3,900.

That is what is called a "growth mindset"; knowing you can learn and do just anything if you put your mind to it.

How to apply this technique to boost your productivity.

As a post or undergraduate student, you can use this technique to boost your productivity and eventually accelerate your learning by doing exactly what Elon Musk does—he is never satisfied with where he is. For instance, you should never settle on a method of learning because it is the one set up for you. You should instead look for better ways to learn. If you are learning law, you don't have to sit in a class for three-to-four years so that you can go for a position in a law firm because that's the way your education system is set.

You can think out of the box and find a law firm that you can work for, even if it's for free, right from when you start learning law. That mixture of theory and experience will increase your knowledge, your productivity, and last but not least, the speed at which you learn law.

Those are the five important techniques of productivity from Elon Musk, which you should most definitely try out. That said, there exists many effective techniques of building productivity out there that you can also use. Some of them include.

✓ **Managing interruptions.**

One of the reasons why you can be unproductive at work is because of interruptions. This can be a friend dropping by the office to visit while you are working, receiving a courtesy call, checking your email, et cetera.

Those unavoidable distractions direct time that you could have otherwise spent on important work, onto trivial things that don't add to your productivity.

So, managing interruptions is one of the techniques you can use to boost your productivity, to do more in less time.

The first thing you can do to manage interruptions is be proactive and tell your colleagues, schoolmates, or people around you of how busy you are and how you need time to focus. Tell them that you will appreciate not being interrupted while you are working, or reading if you are a student.

Moreover, you can manage interruptions by putting your phone on voicemail. This helps you to avoid losing concentration because of a phone call.

In regard to social media, you can form a habit of only checking your social media accounts when you are going home and only checking your emails during a break. That will save you time and increase your productivity.

✓ Have regular breaks.

Here is a fun fact: a 30-second micro break can increase your level of production by 30%! That is how important breaks are to your productivity.

Taking regular breaks when working is a strategy you can use to increase your productivity. The reason why this works so well is because your brain is a muscle, and the more you work it, the more it tires; the regular breaks usually help your brain to rejuvenate and come back sharp and focused.

For instance, a person who works on a computer for four hours continuously does less than a person who works for four hours on a computer but takes ten-minute breaks after every 30 minutes.

✓ Drop your meeting frequencies.

One of the ways you can increase your productivity at work is for you to cut down on your meetings. Meetings are usually made to add value to your work but most of the time, you will find that meetings are just a huge waste of time.

A good example is a manager having a schedule to meet their subordinates three times a week. The truth is, however, that two out of three of these meetings will end up having no urgent agenda, which means you will be wasting one-to-two hours of your time every week.

Therefore, cut down on your meetings and use that time to do something productive.

✓ Apply the two-minute rule.

The two-minute rule enhances productivity in ways that you cannot imagine. The idea behind this rule is that if you come across a task that can be carried out within two minutes or less, do it right away.

This rule helps you to be more productive because completing the task immediately takes you less time than you having to get back to it later. In short, if you are a personal assistant, it is better for you to immediately set that meeting your boss instructed you to set—rather than pushing it aside for later.

If you use the techniques you have just learned, you will increase your productivity and you will be able to learn faster.

The other facet of learning that you need to master as you work on accelerated learning is to improve your memory. Let's discuss how to go about that next.

Chapter 6: Mnemonics: Top 10 Memory Retention Tricks

We all have people in our lives who we've always thought have a better memory than ourselves.

For instance, have you ever encountered a situation where a classmate of yours remembers everything you were taught a week ago in class while you have difficulties just remembering what topic that lesson was from?

This is very common—and the reason why that is so is because there are a good number of people out there who have super memories. They remember things some other people don't think it is possible to remember.

But guess what, having a strong memory is not only meant for a small elite group of people—you can have one too. You can remember things you never thought possible because, just like athletes train themselves to run for long distances, you can also train your brain to hold on to information fast and for a longer time.

So how can you improve your memory?

Improving your level of memory retention is actually easier than you think and this is regardless of whether you want to learn a new language, to study for an exam in school, to learn a new system at work, or you just want to have a sharp memory. All you really need to do is incorporate memorizing techniques that will enhance the efficiency of your memory.

What are these memory techniques, you may ask?

Before we learn the memory techniques, as well as how you can use them, it is important for you to first understand how your brain works when it comes to memory. This will not just enlighten you about the science behind your memory, but it will also show you how some of the memory retention techniques that you will learn actually work.

How Your Brain Recalls Memory

The human brain is a subject of fascination for many. A good number of scientists have carried out studies, trying to understand how humans think and remember. Even though the studies haven't been that successful, we do know a couple of things. One of them is that there are three steps to memory processing; i.e. encoding, storage, and recall.

Here is a brief explanation of each.

Encoding

The first step to creating a new memory is called encoding. Encoding transforms the information or event you have come across into a form that can be stored in your brain.

Here is how it works:

When you go to an event or come across any new information, your brain goes on to consciously register the sounds, physical feeling, images and other sensory details that occur during that particular event.

For example, imagine that you are attending a cooking competition. Your memory of that event will be formed by your sense of smell (the sumptuous aromas from the different types of food), your auditory system (the sound of food cooking and the sound of the chef who is preparing that meal), and your visual system (seeing well-presented foods that look delicious).

In short, every time that you remember the cooking competition, what will come to mind are the foods that you saw, the smells, and the sounds of the cooking.

The effectiveness of your memory depends on the efficiency of your encoding process. The encoding process depends on three factors:

✓ **Content.**

How well you encode information depends on the type of material you come across.

For instance:

1. The higher the degree of familiarity, the easier the encoding.

2. The better the degree of organization in the material, the easier the encoding.

3. The higher the volume of the material, the more difficult it is to encode.

✓ **Environment.**

Environmental factors—although not so much—also affect encoding and your memorization process as a whole. Some of these factors include socio-emotional climate, affection, noise, humidity, and temperature.

These factors may inhibit or stimulate encoding.

✓ **Subjective.**

The subjective factors that are essential when it comes to encoding include your emotional state or current disposition, interests, motivation, health and rest or fatigue.

These factors affect how information is transformed into a memory. Therefore, the better your level of these three factors, the better your chance of encoding information into a memory.

Storing

The second step in the process of creating a new memory is storing. In this step, all those little pieces of information that were encoded in the first step are now preserved in different parts of your brain.

Here is how this happens:

Your neurons, which are the nerve cells in your brain, pass signals among themselves about what you have perceived and as they "talk" to each other, they start building either long term or short term connections. Those neural activities make a memory.

There are two types of memories that are made in your brain and they are both dependent on the duration of retention.

They are:

- **Short-term memory.** This is when your brain stores information temporarily before it dismisses it or transfers it to long-term memory. It is also known as "working memory." A good example of a short-term memory is you remembering your number in a laundry line so that you can know when it's your turn to be served. Once you are called up, your brain then lets the information go.

- **Long-term memory.** This is when your brain stores information that you hold on to for weeks, months, or years. A good example of a long-term memory is you remembering your date of birth or where you first met your partner.

Retrieving

The third and last step in the science of memory is retrieval, which is a process where you access your stored information.

How does this work?

Simple; your brain retrieves a memory by revisiting or replaying the nerve pathways that were created when a certain memory was being formed.

That said, retrieving a memory can occur through recall or through recognition.

Recognition usually involves you associating an object or an event with a previous encounter you have in your memory. For instance, you recognizing a familiar story as the one you are being told or you recognizing a familiar face is a form of recognition.

Recall is a bit more challenging than recognition and this is because in recall, you have to remember an object, event, or fact solely from your memory.

For instance, you try to remember the name of all the countries in Europe. Unlike in recognition—where your memory is triggered by something—in recall, you have to first search and retrieve information from your memory, then go ahead and choose the right information from the vast information that you have retrieved.

The above gives a summary of how your memory works. Now that you are familiar with the science, it is time for you to learn some of the best memorization techniques that use the knowledge you have just learned, to improve your memory.

The most popular of these techniques is mnemonics.

What Are Mnemonic Techniques?

You know those songs and phrases that just seem to be stuck in your memory from nursery through to middle school and high school, like the "ABC" song, or "Thirty days has September, April, June and November ..."? Those were different types of mnemonics.

Mnemonics are basically memory strategies that make remembering information easier. In other words, they are shortcuts that help you remember tedious, difficult, and unfamiliar information.

In this section, you will learn the different types of mnemonics, how they operate and how you can use them to improve your memory.

1. Chunking mnemonic.

Chunking is a mnemonic technique that is amazing when it comes to helping to make huge amounts of information more memorable—particularly for numbers.

How does it work?

To help you understand this, here is a small quiz for you.

Which of these situations is easier for you?

- Memorize this: 233472856420?
- Or memorize this: (2334-7285-6420)?

The second number is definitely the easier one to memorize. That is because it has been grouped—and that is exactly what the chunking technique does.

The chunking technique entails grouping items, finding a pattern in them and organizing the items.

This works wonders for your memory retention, because your brain has evolved to look for patterns and make connections. For instance, the sequence of numbers 1-9-9-8 is a number your brain will prefer to look at as 1998 because it is grouped and it sounds like a year, which is a unique connection that can enable you to remember the number order easily.

The reason why chunking works so efficiently when it comes to mastering long lists of information is because according to research done at the University of Missouri and published in the journal *Proceedings of the National Academy of Sciences*, your brain can hold four different items in your short-term memory, but when you start grouping information, you increase the limit of your working memory to remember more.

With this technique, you can more easily remember things like account numbers and mobile phone numbers.

If you are a reporter in the finance department, this technique can help you to take notes involving numbers quicker, as you would have learned the art of chunking. If you are a student of a foreign language, you can use chunking to learn the language faster, by grouping words into categories like: greetings, food items, plural, singular words, et cetera.

2. Visual mnemonic.

Visualization is an effective retention technique that transforms the information you want to remember into pictures in your brain—that go on to enhance your memory.

There are different ways to use visualization:

- *Employ as many of your senses as possible.*

As you now know, encoding works well when you link a memory with a couple of your senses. For instance, if you want to remember a chemistry procedure, you can picture the whole process as your teacher performed it—but put emphasis on how the chemical smelled, what color the chemicals were and how it felt for you to hold a test tube; was it warm/hot, and smooth perhaps. All that information will make it easier for you to remember what you have learned during that lesson.

- *Animate your images.*

When visualizing, the crazier your images get, the better it is for you to recall them. This is because your brain forms stronger and novel connections that way.

For example, if you are visualizing learning how to drive, the best way to go about it is to envision yourself learning to drive with a Lamborghini. This will improve your chances of remembering faster and more easily.

- *Turn the sounds that you get from names into images.*

Many people have a problem when it comes to remembering the names of people.

However, you can solve this by simply leveraging the power of visualization to turn things around.

How exactly, you may ask?

Well, in this visualization technique, remembering the name of a person becomes easy, as you are instructed to associate the sound of their name with an image. For instance, when a person introduces himself as "Kane," you can connect that name with sugar cane, or the word "can" said with a twist to sound like Kane.

This technique can help you to learn faster, especially if you are a student of history, as history has many names of people and places, from Presidents to war heroes, to historical villains, that you have to learn.

Visual mnemonics help you to encode and store information at a fast rate. You can use this method to retain information in different areas of your life.

For instance, with this method, you can remember someone's name faster and can learn procedures that are related to your job or studies.

3. Acronyms and acrostics mnemonics.

Acronyms and acrostics are perhaps the most used mnemonic techniques.

Acronyms are a type of mnemonic device, which use a letter to represent each phrase or word that you need to remember. For example, think about KFC, which stands for Kentucky Fried Chicken. The acronym KFC is much easier to remember than what it stands for, so by creating it, you increase your chances of remembering the name.

You can use acronyms to remember a math formula you have been taught in school, or a concept you were taught in biology, history, et cetera.

Acrostics are similar to acronyms, with their main difference being that acrostics do not form a new word but instead form a sentence that helps you to remember certain information. I know you've probably heard of the phrase, "My Very Educated Mother Just Served Us Nine Pizzas," which is widely used to remember the order of the nine planets. That is an acrostic mnemonics device, and you can use it to remember almost anything—from your work in class to a shopping list, to the order of operations in your workplace.

4. Music mnemonics.

One of the best strategies you can use to encode and store information—especially long information—is through music.

You may think this is a new concept, but it actually isn't; the nursery rhymes that you still remember mostly centered on this technique! For instance, the "ABC" song for remembering the alphabet, and the "fifty nifty" song for remembering the names of the 50 states in America, are both popular music mnemonics.

Memory retention using music is amazingly effective, because it first provides you with a structure of information and then encourages you to perform repetition, which is how a long-term memory is created. A memory created through music can last for a long time, or even forever.

As a student, you can use music to retain information about what you are learning in class. All you have to do is be creative enough to turn topics—especially those ones that you don't understand—into songs, and let repetition work its magic on you.

A good example is making a song naming all the parts of the body; but the possibilities are endless!

5. Rhyming Peg System.

The peg system is a memory retention technique that uses number rhymes to help you memorize a list of items.

How does it work?

The first step of the peg system is for you to memorize the following list:

- One = bun
- Two = shoe
- Three = tree
- Four = door
- Five = hive
- Six = sticks
- Seven = heaven
- Eight = gate
- Nine = vine
- Ten = hen

This list represents numbers with items that rhyme with it. The images are basically used as a "peg" or "hook," where you can link the information you want to remember.

Let me give you an example: if you want to memorize the planets, after memorizing the peg system rhyming list, you will look at the information you are trying to memorize, and connect it with the associated images. For example, connect Mercury (planet "one") to bun, Venus to shoe, Earth to tree, and so on.

The last step is for you to make a memorable connection between the planets and the images. Like visualizing Mercury being shaped as a bun, Venus as your shoes, and Earth as an oddly shaped tree.

This method may take some time and creativity, but it is very good at recalling information, especially in a specific order.

This method is ideal to almost every stage of your life, because as a student, you can use it to learn sequenced information, and as a shopper, you can use it to recall what was on your grocery list, et cetera.

6. Spaced repetition.

Have you ever heard an interesting story but then twenty minutes later, you couldn't remember what the story was?

Well, that is the nature of forgetting. Your ability to remember usually goes down with the passage of time; and unless you can work on retaining that information, the odds are that you will lose the memory completely.

One of the best strategies you can use to retain the information you have learned is using the "spaced repetition" method.

Let me give you an example: let's say you have learned greetings and courtesy words in Dutch.

The only way you can retain that information is for you to conduct recall sessions of what you know. First, try to remember the Dutch language after two-to-four days.

If you are successful in remembering everything, increase the interval of the recall sessions to eight days, eleven days, fifteen days, three weeks, and so on until that information becomes a part of your long-term memory.

The spaced repetition method helps you to defeat forgetting and works to drill information into your long-term memory. You can use this method to learn a new language or new terms when working in unfamiliar territory—like starting work in a factory for the very first time.

7. The method of Loci.

One of the first mnemonic methods to be discovered was the "Loci" method, which is also one of the most researched.

The Loci method makes you use your imagination to retain information.

The method asks you to do the following;

✓ Visualize a familiar pathway or a room with objects or specific locations along the way. Let's say you are visualizing a room. In front of you, you see a cooker leaning against the wall, you see a fridge in the right-hand corner of the room and a blender placed on the sink that is on the left-hand side of the cooker.

✓ After visualizing this image, the method makes you associate information or facts you have just learned with the objects you saw in the room. So, let's say you want to remember the name of the 50 states in America. You will link one state to one object. For example, the cooker will represent the state of Florida, the fridge will be Atlanta, and the blender will be Texas.

✓ The last step is re-visualizing. Here, you are supposed to re-visualize the room and move around, recalling the states you associated with the objects. For instance, when you see the cooker, say "That is Florida," and go on associating the other objects with the states. You will use the same technique when you want to recall the 50 states.

There are endless ways and situations where you can use this method to recall information. For example, as an IT specialist you can use it to recall a couple of steps in the process of making software, and as a student you can use it to remember countries and their capital cities.

8. The linking system.

The linking system, also known as "chaining," is a mnemonic technique that helps you to remember a huge amount of information by you linking it together.

How does it work?

This method makes you develop a story or image that gathers and connects pieces of information that you need to remember. For instance, let's say you want to remember to buy the following things in the farmers market: mango, tomatoes, bananas, kale, cabbages and broccoli. Use the linking system to create a short story like; Jimmy went to a restaurant looking for a banana snack. When he reached there, he found me eating a salad made of kale, tomatoes and broccoli. He changed his mind and ordered a cabbage salad and mango juice.

The more details you add to the linking method, the better your chances of recalling the information you want.

This method is great for remembering shopping lists—but also for other important information you may be learning during your accelerated learning journey.

Those eight techniques are amazingly effective and can help you boost your memory to levels you never imagined possible. Next, we will discuss how to focus efficiently and ultimately learn fast.

Chapter 7: Maximize Your Focus: 12 Ways to Focus More Effectively

On a scale of 1-10, how good do you think you would rate your focus when studying or when doing your work?

If you are really honest with yourself, your answer is likely to be between 1-5 and this is purely because the world as you know it today is not the same as the world you knew ten or fifteen years ago.

Today, we are faced with all manner of distractions that make it hard to focus.

Let me explain:

A few decades ago, our forefathers used to wake up early in the morning, prepare themselves (father, mother, and kids), head out for their daily commitments and only hold proper conversations in the evening when they were back from their respective commitments. There was no way they could contact each other in between, during their respective activities. The same applied to their friends, relatives, customers, and other parties; when everyone entered their cubicles or classes, et cetera, there was nothing to distract them other than maybe colleagues within their office.

The situation is different in today's world.

In today's world, with mobile phones, emails, social media, instant messengers, and the likes, it is so easy to catch up with friends and even strangers through messaging them or visiting their social media profiles.

This means that while you may part ways with your family in the morning, you still can stay in touch with them all day through different communication channels. While this is good for staying in touch, it has its downsides and one of the biggest downsides is the fact that it steals your focus, to a point where your productivity goes down.

The time that was once spent learning or working is today shared between that and the distractions from the "new technology"—if you can call it that. This is supported by a discovery that David Rock, the author of *Your Brain at Work: Strategies for Overcoming Distraction, Regaining Focus, and Working Smarter All Day Long*, made—that most people only focus on their work for approximately six hours per week. Shocking, right?

So how do you manage to lose so much focus like that?

To know that, you need to first understand how you concentrate.

How Do You Concentrate?

Focus can be described as a thinking skill, which allows you to attend to a task and maintain that attention and effort until you complete the task.

So how do you normally focus?

When you want to focus on something, let's say a picture; what normally happens is that your brain takes the visual information in the picture and then processes it.

Once the picture is clear, your brain moves toward the one aspect you want to direct your attention to, e.g. a flower in the photograph. The more you are captivated by that flower, the more your perception of what is around it changes. For instance, if the flower in the photograph is next to vegetables, the vegetables fade as your interest in the flower increases, giving you a heightened ability to ignore any outside stimuli.

Why do you lose concentration?

Losing your concentration is a normal and natural thing. In fact, it is a process meant to keep you safe. Your brain is made to disrupt you and bring your attention to things that might need it—like a fire in a building.

Naturally, your focus should break when there is a reward or danger. The disadvantage that comes with breaking focus is that it takes you up to 25 minutes for you to refocus on what you were doing before. That is the undeniable cost of interruptions.

Here is a surprising fact for you: you have the ability to focus on a task for two hours before needing 20-30 minutes of rest to recharge!

The question now is; why don't you always live up to that potential?

The truth of the matter is that it is really hard for you to hit those levels of concentration, especially in the eight-to-nine hours you spend working or studying in a day.

Here are some of the reasons that make it hard for you to concentrate for two hours straight.

- ✓ **Stress.**

Have you ever noticed how hard it is for you to concentrate on a task after a big fight that you have had with your friend, family member, or colleague?

That is because stress is one of the factors that affect your focus.

Stress short-circuits your important cognitive functions by becoming a priority point of focus in your brain.

As such, to get your focus back, you need to deal with the stress first and then your focus can be directed to the right place.

- ✓ **Multitasking.**

Multitasking can easily make you lose focus and only makes you end up accomplishing less.

This is because when you do more than one thing at a time you are not able to give each task 100% of your focus. And without sufficient focus, you may end up ignoring your cognitive needs, because dealing with a wide range of distractions has become more satisfying to you than your work.

✓ **Doing what you don't like.**

If you are not emotionally and mentally involved in a task, you lack the excitement to give it 100% of your attention. And as you may guess, when that happens, you become very susceptible to losing concentration.

For instance, if you don't love writing but you force yourself to anyway, then any text alert, music, or email notification can make you want to shift your focus.

So how exactly can you break these bad habits and build your focus to get more stuff done? Here are ten powerful techniques that will help you to improve your focus, which will automatically accelerate your learning ability.

1. **Pre-commit yourself to a task.**

This simply entails you making a commitment to a task before you start working on that task. How will this help you improve your focus?

There are two ways you can use pre-commitment to enhance your focus:

- You can use some sort of harsh consequence that will bind you to finish a task before you even start it. Let's say that you are a writer and you want to write a 100-page book in 30 days, which means you will need to write three pages per day. You can set a pre-commitment consequence of you not taking your morning coffee if you don't hit your daily target. That said, the consequence must be something that will really get to you if it happens. In this example, you must really love coffee for you to put it as your consequence. The cruelty of that consequence will motivate you to stay focused on the task at hand, as you wouldn't want to suffer without your morning caffeine hit.

  If coffee does not work for you, perhaps money will; give your friend or "accountability partner" $100 (for example) that they will use as they please—or give it to a charity organization that deals with something you are against. The thought of losing money because of not doing what you promised to do will keep you on your toes, with no excuses.

• You can pre-commit yourself to doing one task by eliminating your ability to do anything else at that particular time. As you know by now, working on a computer exposes you to a multitude of distractions. That said, if you block your email, Facebook, Twitter, LinkedIn—et cetera—and uninstall PC games and the video player on your computer, you will end up with a device that is free of distractions. You could even disconnect your device from the internet if what you are doing does not involve searching for information online. Don't stop there; there are powerful apps/software that can help you to do that: like SelfControl for Mac, Freedom, Stay Focusd Google Chrome extension, LeechBlock Mozilla Firefox add on, FocusMe, Cold Turkey Blocker for Windows and Mac, RescueTime for all OSs and many others. By using these tools, you will put yourself in a position where the only thing you can do with your computer is work. That will automatically skyrocket your focus.

So, the strategy here is for you to either cut off all distractions or set tough consequences for not doing the work before you start your task.

2. Meditation and mindfulness.

Meditation and mindfulness are two practices that can improve your focus immensely.

One of the reasons why you lose focus when working is because you seek short-term pleasures like chatting with your friend online and many other things.

What meditation does is train you not to seek short-term pleasures.

Here is how:

With meditation, you have to find a quiet place, sit in a comfortable position, close your eyes and focus your attention on your normal breathing for a specific amount of time.

While in this state, meditation somewhat allows you to "embrace boredom" without you feeling bothered by it. So, when you practice meditation frequently, your brain slowly learns to be less fascinated by short term pleasures.

Your body also receives a satisfying calmness, which makes it easier for you to work on activities that produce long-term pleasures without being distracted. That is what makes it an amazing technique when it comes to improving your focus.

To try this technique, register for a meditation class, meditate frequently and watch your focus grow. You could even learn how to meditate by watching a few YouTube videos.

3. Create a "not-to-do" list.

The concentration problem that you have does not usually come from you not knowing what to do—but from you not knowing what *not* to do.

Be honest for a minute; how many times have you had an assignment but when you are 30 minutes into the assignment, you get an urge to check your friends' Facebook status, or an urge to ask your colleague something that is totally unrelated to your work?

Then you go ahead and tell yourself that the few minutes you spend on this distraction won't matter much?

This is a common issue for almost all of us, but unfortunately, it only fuels the bad habit of lack of focus.

So, what do you do about it?

Well, the fastest way to solve the problem is to have a "not-to-do" list—the opposite of a "to-do" list.

To create one, you need to first think of all the distractions that provide you with short-term pleasures, like chatting with friends, calling your family, or updating your social media handles.

Write those distractions down on a piece of paper and either stick it to your computer or place it anywhere else where you can see it often—somewhere visible during your working hours.

The list will remind you of what *not* to do, something that will effectively improve your focus and save you all of that time you would usually waste on distractions.

4. Decide what is worth your attention.

Thanks to technology, an average day is full of distractions. And the confusing thing about this is that those distractions are sometimes "good" distractions.

For instance, your friend calling to inform you about a date change for a meeting you were going to attend, is somewhat of a "good" distraction. That said, it is impossible for you to get anything done if you are splitting your attention between several good distractions.

So, what do you need to do to regain your focus?

The answer is simple: you need to decide what is worth your attention. For example, is taking that twenty-minute call from your friend really worth the lost productivity?

It's probably not, which means you should ignore it and continue concentrating on what is really important. Have people send emails or voice messages instead of you having to talk for far too long when it is completely unnecessary.

You should make a habit of questioning the importance of a distraction compared to what you are doing.

How should you go about this, you may ask?

The best way is for you to dedicate a few minutes before starting a task to think just how important that task is to you.

Let me give you an example; if you are watching a tutorial to learn a topic you didn't understand in school, you can tell yourself what you are about to watch is going to improve your understanding of the current topic, as well as future subjects related to it.

Once you define the importance of what you are about to do, it becomes very hard for you to refocus your attention to less important things; like friendly phone calls, Facebook notifications, and a colleague's story, among other things.

5. Concentrate on one thing at a time.

One of the reasons why you don't always focus effectively is because as a child, the school system only told you to concentrate— but no one bothered to tell you how.

To learn how to concentrate, you first need to understand how your mind works—and the best explanation is from a monk's perspective.

Assume that for one minute, your awareness is a movable torch and your mind is a huge dark place with different sections within it, like a section of happiness, of playing, of anger, of food, and so on. Throughout the day, the torch swings to different sections of your mind, and when it does, it lights that section up and makes your mind conscious of it. If it moves to happiness, you become happy, and if it moves to anger you become angry.

The secret to having improved focus is learning how to keep your concentration—i.e. the torch—directed toward one section for a long period. For instance, if you are reading a book, this technique dictates that you don't allow anything, including music or your friends, to move your torch to another section of your brain. However, if these distractions manage to get your attention, you should not get agitated or frustrated—simply refocus your torch on reading.

To be able to concentrate on one thing at a time, always cultivate your discipline of keeping your awareness on whatever you are doing. If you are walking your dog, keep your awareness on walking; if you are talking to a friend, keep your awareness on that conversation and nothing else.

6. Grow your focus gradually.

To enhance your focus to a level that you desire, you need to work on this and grow it gradually.

- To apply this technique, you will first need to know your concentration levels. You can do this by trying to perform what you do for the majority of your day, for example, making computer software or managing a project, and then time yourself as you do it to see how long your concentration lasts. Let's say for instance that you learn your concentration span for writing a book is ten minutes.

- The next step will be for you to try to increase that concentration to fifteen minutes. The best way to do that is to take part in a relaxation session, like yoga or meditation, five-to-ten minutes before you start writing again. A relaxation session can be very effective for increasing your focus, so after you do this, your concentration will definitely increase.

- The last step will be you making this technique of growing your concentration an everyday habit.

7. Re-engineer information to make it interesting.

To improve your focus, you need to keep your mind interested in whatever you are doing. One way is to do different things with the information that you are receiving.

For instance, if you are studying catering, you can enhance your focus when studying by incorporating your other senses into your work. So instead of you reading about baking techniques, you can try to learn them practically. As you cook, you will feel the texture of different ingredients, smell the aroma of the cakes, and finally see how beautiful the cake comes out.

By doing this you will use a variety of methods to translate the information you are receiving. This activates different parts of your brain, something that will create more neural connections and automatically heighten your focus.

Therefore, whenever you want to have a higher level of focus on something that you are doing, you should think of ways you can involve your other senses.

8. Take short breaks.

One of the easiest techniques you can use to enhance your focus is taking frequent but short breaks when working.

You might not know this but one of the reasons why you lose focus is because you have worked over a long period.

When you work without resting, the thinking part of your brain—the prefrontal cortex—which is also the part that deals with focus, gets tired and your focus goes down.

Taking frequent breaks gives your prefrontal cortex time to recharge and renew. This gives it more energy and motivation later when you resume working.

So, set at least five-to-ten minute breaks after working for 30 minutes.

9. Doodling.

Have you ever sat in a long lecture and found yourself drawing things on the edge of your book? That is called "doodling." From afar, doodling seems like a useless thing to do but what you might not know is that this technique helps you stay focused.

How?

Your brain usually bounces between moments of activity and moments of inactivity. When your brain is active, your eyes are able to focus in any direction and the visual information is received in the right place.

When you stop paying attention, your brain goes into a default mode or it becomes inactive. In this case, your brain goes into a relaxation mode where you can't notice what is going on in the environment that you are in.

Doodling helps you stay focused because it helps your brain not to go into default mode where can't receive any information from your surroundings. So next time you find yourself doodling in class, don't stop, because it will help you learn faster.

10. Eliminate distractions.

Earlier, we learned how to make pre-commitments to avoid getting distracted. As much as that is helpful, you still have external distractions that can affect your focus. Some of these distractions include music, friends popping in, and co-workers striking up conversations.

The best way to eliminate external distractions is to come up with a list of potential issues and then find a way to deal with them.

For instance, if you want to create a computer application, the two items in your external distraction list will probably be co-workers popping in and email notifications. You can deal with these distractions by finding an empty room that is far away from your co-workers. You can also tell your friends and co-workers not to disturb you. On the part of emails, you can disconnect your internet. That way, you will have created an environment that encourages pure focus.

To accelerate your learning, you need to know what you now know—which is: how to learn in a super-fast way, how to speed read, how to be extra productive, how to have an enhanced memory retention and how to increase your focus.

But as much as all of that is important, it is also critical for you to master your intention and the "success mindset," which is what we will learn next.

Chapter 8: Mastering Intention and the Success Mindset

You might not know this, but mastering your intention and your success mindset is essential to you accelerating your learning.

How so, you may wonder?

Well, this chapter will teach you the impact that intention and a success mindset have on learning, and the steps you can take to achieve both.

Let's start with mastering intention.

Mastering Intention

The world we live in today is an action-packed life where most of us think about what we can do, how we can do more, and what we can do next.

As you might guess, this mentality has led many of us to always be busy jumping from one activity to another; and as you learned earlier, jumping from one distraction to another.

Be honest for a minute.

When was the last time you sat down and did nothing but just think? You probably don't remember, right?

Many of us are simply not intentional with our thinking; we just move through life in some sort of "autopilot" mode. We are never intentional in our thinking and this is maybe because we don't see it as an important activity—which it is. In fact, if you think being busy is productive, you should try intentional thinking; many great leaders throughout history created outstanding results through utilizing their thinking time, with good examples being Albert Einstein and Henry Ford. Henry Ford once said: "Thinking is the hardest work there is, which is probably the reason so few engage in it."

Many of us don't really think about what we are doing; we operate on autopilot mode; i.e. reacting to what is happening in the environment we are in, as opposed to directing our thoughts so that we don't just react. For example, as a student, you can go to class to learn but end up playing board games with your classmates—simply because that is the activity that is happening in class and since you are on autopilot, you go with the flow.

So, what is the danger of you being on autopilot?

The danger is that letting the autopilot take over makes it hard to keep our limiting beliefs and impulses in check; we simply go with the flow, something that can easily make it hard to accelerate our learning.

How can you check these impulses then? The answer is through practicing intentional thinking.

What Is Intentional Thinking?

Intentional thinking is simply spending some time thinking, without interruptions from your phone, TV, your family, and friends. It entails you just thinking about your life, your current thought, your plans, goals, your problems, how to solve them, et cetera.

But doesn't that sound like a goal setting process? Well, intentional thinking and setting a goal are two different things. Goal setting is about achievement while intentional thinking is about awareness. For instance, setting a goal makes you want to score an "A" in math, but intentional thinking makes you want to understand math more.

How Does Intentional Thinking Impact Learning?

Your thoughts usually have the power to lead you to a path of success or a path of failure when it comes to learning.

Here is how:

When you are on autopilot, i.e. when you don't practice intentional thinking, you react to life. This means you follow just any thought that comes your way.

For instance, many of us have grown up being told that math is a hard subject that is only suited to those who are "gifted in math." If you don't practice intentional thinking, you could easily grow up believing what you were told and true to your belief, math becomes hard for you. This is because how you think about something dictates how you feel, which in turn creates like-minded actions.

On the other hand, when you tap into the power of intentional thinking, what normally happens is that *you take control of your life by starting to live your life, instead of letting life live you.* This automatically brings light to your learning experience and this is because you become aware of your thoughts and you become willing to challenge them. If you take the just mentioned example for instance, intentional thinking makes you question the notion that math is hard. This leads to you investigating and trying to find if there is any proof that math is hard. The probable outcome will be you finding out that the notion math is hard is just a myth.

That's how intentional thinking impacts learning; it makes you question all the myths that make learning challenging. This transforms you into an open-minded person, which is the right attitude to have when it comes to learning.

Ultimately, you end up deriving a number of benefits from being an intentional thinker.

1. Intentional thinking helps you to develop new perspectives.

As you have learned, you have limiting beliefs that are buried deep in your subconscious that can limit the way you view learning, as well as the way you learn. One of the benefits of intentional thinking is how it lets you examine your limiting beliefs like math is hard; reading is boring; failing an exam means you are dumb, et cetera. Once you examine these beliefs, you come to the realization that they are not true. You get to know that math is not hard—it just requires you to be keen with how numbers work; reading is not boring—all you need is to work on your concentration; and failing exams does not mean you are dumb—it just means you didn't prepare enough to pass for the exam.

This gives you a new perspective of your limiting beliefs, which transforms you into a person who is more open to reality and less held up by limiting past ideas.

2. It makes you a solution-oriented person.

When you know your limiting beliefs were just twisted lies, the other benefit you get is that you become a solution-oriented person. In short, you become open minded to possibilities. For instance, you stop seeing math as a hard subject and try to find ways that can help math work for you. You could think of looking for a tutor or joining a math club, or you might decide to have an open mind toward math teachings. In simple terms, intentional thinking turns you into a person that tries to seek solutions to your difficulties when it comes to learning.

3. It gets you deeply involved in your own learning.

If you are a student, intentional thinking can help you to get deeply involved in your own learning, which improves your understanding greatly.

How?

One way that you can use intentional thinking is in summarizing what you have just learned in class. The process of summarizing gets you deep into your learning.

4. It helps you connect old knowledge to new knowledge.

When you think about what you learn, you sometimes get to activate old knowledge that relates to your new knowledge, something which can greatly help you to understand a certain topic better.

For instance, if you are a trainee nurse learning how to handle a wound and you think intentionally, you might come across a memory created a few years ago where you attended a first aid seminar. With that memory, you can connect your new knowledge with the old knowledge and get to understand the topic you are learning better.

5. It helps you to be organized.

Intentional thinking can help you to think about your studies and plan for them. For instance, it can make you come up with a revision timetable where each day you focus on a particular subject.

So when you go to class and find the lecturer is absent, the first thing in your mind won't be to play board games simply because that's what is being done by your classmates, but to study for the subject you have set out to study on that particular day.

How Can You Be Intentional in Your Thinking?

Being intentional in your thinking is very important, especially when creating good learning habits. Here is the perfect path you can use to set your intentions.

Step 1: Make a ritual.

Creating a ritual or setting your intention should be your first step. Choose a time—in the morning if possible—where you can take five-minutes to set your intention. This can be immediately after you wake up or before you go out to school.

Step 2: Write down your intention.

For that five-minutes in the morning, think and write down your day's intention, preferably on a journal you can use to refer to later. Your intention should be specific, creative, and a high-level dream—you should aim higher than where you are currently at.

Try to see what you want to change. If you want to improve your concentration in class, you can say, *"I will have top-notch concentration in my classes."* If you want to have better understanding, you can set your intention to be, *"I will try to use my imagination and senses to improve my understanding."*

The process of writing these down connects your mind and your intentions, which automatically enhances them even more.

Step 3: Make yourself aware of your intentions.

As you go about your daily activities, you should try to be aware of your intentions by thinking about them. The best way to do this is for you to set a few reminders on your phone each day to remind you when to revisit your intentions. The frequent reminders will help shift the pathways of your brain.

Step 4: Celebrate your achievements.

The next step to setting and following your intentions is to celebrate your achievements. If you managed to concentrate for twenty minutes, which is ten minutes more than you usually do, celebrate that victory and celebrate also the fact that you are starting to be aware of your intentions. This will automatically motivate you to do more.

Step 5: Start slowly and be patient.

For you to fully master your intentions, it will take some time to adjust. So, it is advisable for you to start with a small intention like saying *"I want to always be on time in class."* Give yourself 20-30 days to adjust, then move to the next intention. After making your intention a habit, you should take some time to reflect and appreciate your progress.

Now that you've learned how to set your intention, next, the focus will be how to build a success mindset.

Success Mindset

Your thoughts determine your success in life.

As much as being intentional with your thoughts is important, it doesn't make sense if your thoughts are not from a success mindset.

Here is the deal; your thoughts are usually the roots of your destiny. This is because:

Your thoughts turn into words, words turn into actions, action habits, habits turn to character and character turns into your desti

As you can see, how your life turns out starts with your thoughts, which means it's the best place to work on creating a successful mindset.

Basically, there are two ways you can think.

- **Negatively.** Negative thinking tells your brain you can't do whatever you are supposed to do. For instance, if you are having an exam, your mind will tell you that you will fail that exam.

- **Positively.** Positive thinking always tells your brain that you can do something. You *can* pass an exam and you can be the best at what you do in life.

Positive thinking is the one that promotes a success mindset—and that is the mindset you need to have if you are to set intentions that work. For instance, you can intend to concentrate more in class all you want but if you don't have a success mindset, you won't succeed in your intention. That is why cultivating a success mindset is important.

So How Can You Cultivate a Success Mindset When Setting an Intention?

You can achieve a success mindset by doing the following:

✓ **Make a mantra.**

Setting a mantra is one way you can create a successful mindset when setting an intention.

Let's say your intention is to concentrate more in class. Here is how to use a mantra to enhance that intention:

First, take some time and think of what you really want. The probable answer is you want to pass your end of semester exam and that's why you want to concentrate more in your learning.

Second, think about all the ways you are subconsciously blocking yourself from your goal. One of the things blocking you might be the fear of not being good enough. Another one might be you thinking you will never make it.

Third, after making yourself aware of those thoughts that block you, slowly try to tune them out with a positive mantra. For example, *"I am good enough, I have within me the ability to do anything and I am going to pass my exam."* Repeat this positive mantra to yourself until you get the determination to accomplish your goal of increasing your concentration and passing your exam. For the mantra to be more effective, you can repeat it on a daily basis, until your mindset grows stronger.

✓ **Practice being positive.**

Many people tend to be very negative about the outcome of their efforts. The reason for that might be to not get their own hopes—or those of friends and family—up. However, this ends up working against them because they only get what they project.

For you to have a successful mindset that can make the art of intentional thinking even more powerful, you must change your mindset to a more positive one. You can do this by practicing how to focus on the positives in your life.

Set a time, maybe in the morning or at night, where you celebrate your positive achievements for that day. This makes you believe in yourself more. For instance, if you are a third-year student and you look at the positives in your life, you will realize it's a big achievement for you to be in your third year at university. Celebrating this fact will make you believe you are great and that will motivate you to believe you can also achieve the thing you deeply desire, which might be something like graduating with honors.

✓ **Imagine you have accomplished your goal.**

When you set an intention that says you want to improve how you perform in your German class and the exam is five weeks from today, there is a huge chance that your intention may fade due to the many challenges you will face in the following five-week period.

One way you can create a successful mindset that will push your intention until the end is you practicing imaginary success.

Here is how it goes:

Close your eyes and imagine yourself having passed your exams.

Stay in that happy space for a while, as you tap into those happy emotions.

That activity strengthens your mindset, because it makes you feel that achieving your goal is possible. Do this a couple of times a week and you will grow a success mindset.

✓ **Share the intention you have with a friend.**

Having someone you are accountable to can turn things around as far as moving forward is concerned. So instead of simply "sitting" on your intentions silently, tell a friend (or several friends) what your intentions are and ask them to follow up with you to know your progress.

What that does is create a team of people ready to hold you accountable. Therefore, if you said you will turn your aquaponics theory lesson into a practical one, you will need to do exactly that because you now have people who are watching you. That accountability will help you to develop a success mindset.

Intentional thinking with a success mindset plays a huge role when it comes to you accelerating your learning. This is because it sets the right mood in your brain, which boosts your desire to accelerate your learning.

Now that you know that, the next step is for you to look at some high performers who are successful in their fields and see what lessons you can draw from them that will help you in your quest to accelerate your learning.

Chapter 9: High Performer Brain Hacks

What is that one thing that you, your boss, the brightest person in your school, and the richest person in the world have in common? One word: BRAINS!

The question now is, if we all have a brain; why is it that today, there are people who are wealthier and more successful than you in their careers, education, and other facets of life?

The main difference is mindset.

High achievers and high performers succeed in what they do because they have winning mindsets. This chapter is going to introduce you to four high performers and the mindsets they use to be successful, which is what you must also use to be successful in accelerating your learning.

Tony Robbins

Tony Robbins is a motivational guru who is mostly known for providing advice to US presidents and Fortune 500 CEOs. He gives multi-day seminars where he speaks continuously for ten hours. Through his efforts, Robbins has been able to launch a multi-million-dollar franchise off the practice of helping people like you become their best selves.

You can learn a lot from Tony's mindset to better your life. Let's discuss three of these lessons:

1. **Change the story you tell yourself.**

One of the powerful mindsets that Tony has been living by and teaching his audience over the years is that you need to change the story you tell yourself to one that is positive and progressive. He believes that if you can do only that, then you can have and be exactly what you wish to be.

To quote Tony, *"Success in life is 80% psychology and 20% mechanics—what you do doesn't matter if you aren't in the right mindset."*

Tony Robbins has been able to succeed in different areas of his life because in his mind, he doesn't believe in limiting vocabularies like "I can't." He, instead, tells himself powerful and positive stories, which lead to him having a life full of opportunities.

The question is; how many times have you ever found yourself saying things like, "I am not the focused type" or "high achievers in my class are geniuses and learning comes easy to them"?

To be successful in whatever you do—and especially in accelerating learning—you must develop a mindset like the one Tony Robbins has, of changing the story you tell yourself.

How should you do it?

The first thing you need to do is to investigate the stories you tell yourself to see if they are true. You probably have a lot of stories you tell yourself but let's assume one of them is that you think the high performers in your class are geniuses and learning comes easy to them.

You need to investigate that story and find out if they are geniuses, and if learning comes easy to them.

Here is how you investigate:

- Choose four-to-five classmates who are high performers.
- Arrange for a meeting with them.
- Question them to know why they are successful in class.

You will be surprised to learn that those high achievers in your class work really hard on their focus and their ability to understand and remember concepts.

Right there and then, you will know all it takes to be successful is working hard at your studies.

Investigating your story is important because it makes you discover the beliefs that limit your ability to succeed and that enables you to move to the next step, which is changing that story to one that encourages you to succeed.

In your case, you can change your story to: *"I can be the best performer in class if I work hard on my focus and my ability to remember what I have been taught in class."*

2.   Direct your focus to what you want.

One of Tony Robbins's quotes that is a favorite to many is; *"where focus goes, energy flows."*

Where your focus is directed mostly determines how successful or unsuccessful you are in life. If you wake up one morning and the first thing you think about is what you don't have, what you haven't accomplished or how bad your life is, you will spend the whole day attracting and manifesting your negative thoughts.

For instance, if you don't have a love life, you will see a lot of love birds around you, to remind you what you are missing. If you wake up thinking how bad your life is, you will probably go on to have a horrible day that resonates with your thoughts.

What Tony says is that the more you think about something, the more that thing—whatever it may be—sticks to your mind and ends up dictating your day because it is the direction that your energy flows toward.

Let's do a simple test to prove that.

Follow everything that I am about to tell you. Ready? Let's go.

- Don't think of a yellow car.
- Don't think of a big yellow car.
- Do not think of a dirty yellow car stuck in mud.

What did you think about? A yellow car, a big yellow car and a dirty yellow car stuck in mud, right? That is despite you being told *"do not"* think about this.

This just shows that energy flows where focus goes.

That said, Tony has helped a lot of people to succeed in different areas of life by teaching a mindset created by habit which is; *always direct your focus to what you want.*

For instance, instead of thinking how negative your life is each morning as a student, start your day by thinking about the positives you want in your life. You could say things like "I am the brightest student in school, I am going to have a nice day today and I will understand all the concepts I am taught in class today." This will help you to succeed in school as well as in learning fast because your energy will flow toward the positives you have just focused on.

Focusing on what you want motivates you to do anything possible to get it, including being creative in learning to achieve your goal of accelerating your learning.

3.   Position your body for success.

Tony Robbins has a very crazy ritual that he performs every morning. When he wakes up in the morning, he jumps into freezing cold water to wake his body up. It's not a pleasurable ritual at all but Robbins believes that whatever the body does, the mind follows suit. So, by him waking up his body, his mind wakes up too. This process is called "state changing."

As a student, you need to do what Robbins does to accelerate your learning.

Does that mean you jumping into icy cold water? No. It means you should apply the state changing concept to help you in your learning. How will you do that? One way you can do this is by you preparing your body for success.

Here is how:

- Form a habit of sitting upright in class with a smile on your face. This will influence you to be more positive. When you are positive, you tend to have that internal motivation to do more of whatever you are doing, and in your case, that is learning.

- You can also form a habit of dressing like a successful student. This involves always being neat and smart. When you dress smart, you feel good and your mindset is transformed into a positive one. That positive wave will affect your learning, as you will find yourself wanting to match how good you feel with a good performance, which means you working hard.

Robert Kiyosaki

Robert Kiyosaki is known for being the author of the bestselling book, *Rich Dad Poor Dad*.

Here are three great mindsets you can take from him.

1. Look out to gain experience.

Just like most people, Kiyosaki didn't have much money when he started his career. Nevertheless, he believes that experience is what made him become as successful as he is today.

The first investment property he bought as a real estate investor was a small condominium in Hawaii that was going for $18,000. Using his credit card, Kiyosaki paid a deposit of $2,000 on the property and even though he admitted that was not a wise move, he appreciated the deal because that was one of the experiences that made him the great real estate investor that he is today.

The moral of the story is; you can never learn to ride a bicycle by reading a book, or learn how to swim by watching a YouTube video. You need to hop on the bicycle and learn through experience and the same goes for swimming—you need to get into the water and learn how to swim.

Learning in general especially accelerated learning is no different from swimming and riding a bike. You can never be a good and fast learner if you only read books; you need to mix your book knowledge with seeking out experience like attending group discussions, seminars and applying your knowledge in real life situations. If you are an art student—for example—paint or draw something. Ask your friends for opinions and even try to set an art exhibition just to get a feel of what people want.

Indeed, you can learn faster if you have a mindset of always seeking to gain experience.

2. Do not be afraid to lose.

Kiyosaki has always made it clear to his audience that he was not an overnight success. He always says he believes he is where he is today because of the many failures he had in his businesses. He says his failures were lessons he needed to learn to go to the next level.

Kiyosaki believes you should embrace failure and not fear it because it is the only way you will learn. In his talks, he always compares how a baby learns to walk with how we learn different things in life.

When babies learn to walk, they do it by standing up, falling down and then standing right up again. Normally, the babies learn more during their falls and that is why no one condemns them for falling.

What is shocking to him though is how society and schools have conditioned you to believe failing is a bad thing. Kiyosaki says that when you are afraid to make a mistake, you usually let your fear of failure stop you from learning.

To accelerate your learning, you need to cultivate the mindset of embracing failure. Instead of you thinking you are dumb for failing your exams, think of it as an opportunity for you to be aware of how much you don't know about a particular topic or topics—then work on those topics again and again until you understand and master them.

3. Be bold.

One of the mindsets that Kiyosaki always talks about and lives by is being bold. In the early 90s, when the property markets in Arizona and Phoenix were terrible, Kiyosaki made deals to buy houses in bankruptcy lawyer's offices and outside courts. Through this method, he would buy a house valued at $750,000 for $200,000 or less. He would later sell them for $600,000, which helped him make a profit of almost $1.9 million when he sold all those properties he had bought.

In the real world, it's not the smart people who get ahead but the bold ones. The profit Kiyosaki made from his real estate deals in Phoenix and Arizona was because he was bold enough to take the risk of buying in a terrible property market.

In accelerated learning, the mindset of being bold is a mindset that can help you get ahead and succeed. This is because accelerated learning needs some level of boldness in almost every area of it. For instance, as a student, you need to be aware of how you are doing in class. Look at yourself honestly and come up with the weaknesses that make you an average learner.

Do something about those weaknesses; a good example is you looking for someone who can assist you to strengthen your knowledge and in your areas of weaknesses. To do that needs a bold mindset.

Boldness also plays a big role in accelerated learning when it comes to failure.

How?

Following accelerated learning does not mean you won't fail a couple of times along the way. Failure is inevitable and you will probably fail at speed reading or the art of memory retention and right there and then, you will need a bold mindset that will help you to look at that failure as a learning opportunity.

Gary Vaynerchuk

Gary Vaynerchuk is an American entrepreneur, speaker and internet personality and *New York Times* bestselling author. He is the CEO of VaynerMedia, which is a full-service advertising agency.

Here are three mindsets that you can adopt from Gary Vaynerchuk.

1. Aim for happiness.

One of the messages that Vaynerchuk popularizes a lot is the message that you should always aim for happiness in whatever you are doing. His definition of happiness is you being able to do what you want at all times. He says when you aim for happiness, the activities that you do become easier and effortless to you because you are doing something that you love. That said, this does not mean you quit every activity that does not make you happy now; it means you working through tasks you don't like because they are leading to an outcome or a lifestyle change that you do like.

Aiming for happiness is a mentality that can help you a lot when it comes to accelerated learning.

Here is how:

The process of accelerated learning can sometimes be a not-so-rosy experience. For instance, for you to improve your focus, you must eliminate distractions in your workplace or at school. Some of these distractions, which include music and social media sites, are things that have been a part of you for a long time, which means it will be a painful process to eliminate them.

Now if what you are doing isn't something that you really want, it becomes very hard for you to sacrifice all those distractions that you like for something that you don't like that much.

So, what can you do to make it easier for you to eliminate the distractions you have, even though what you are doing currently is not that pleasing to you?

The answer is: you need to write down all the things that you will gain if you achieve the goal you are chasing after. If you are studying law, write down everything good you will get from being a lawyer and stick that piece of paper on your laptop or on your desk. By you constantly seeing what you stand to gain, eliminating those "attractive" distractions like watching the new Spiderman movie will be easier for you even though studying at that point in time doesn't seem pleasant, because your head will be aiming for the long-term goodies that you stand to gain.

2. Have some gratitude.

One of the successful mindsets that Gary Vaynerchuk says you should adopt to succeed in different areas of your life is the mindset of practicing gratitude to yourself.

This might come as a surprise to you, but the things you focus your attention on are the things you end up valuing more, and these are also the things that manifest in your life.

Therefore, when you do not practice gratitude and you continuously feel like you are useless and stupid, your mind will end up valuing your thoughts, which will translate to them being a reality for you.

Vaynerchuk teaches you to practice gratitude because when you do, you turn your attention to the things that you value and appreciate—like your gifts, your abilities, family and friends. In short, your mind shifts to you seeing the blessings in your life and that is what later manifests in your life.

This mindset can help you succeed in accelerating your learning.

How?

Let's say you want to master the art of speed reading. The first few trials of reading fast will most likely be substandard. You may have targeted to read two books in a week and end up reading half a book in a week. The mindset of you showing yourself gratitude will help you keep going because you will focus on the positives, like how you are now reading faster than you did before.

3. Be excited each and every day.

According to Gary Vaynerchuk, for you to have a mindset that leads to success, you need to be excited each morning because it's a new day and you have another chance to play, whether that is taking another step toward your goal or you going out to finalize a deal you have worked on for a long time.

He says you being fired up in the morning provides you with a vigor that builds momentum and help you to make a mark in whatever activity you are doing. This kind of mindset is important when using accelerated learning because it provides you with an everyday push to do better.

For instance, if you are working on a two year project to build a mobile application that will control the business of a whole transport system in your country, the motivation of you being a part of a team that will make a groundbreaking application will push your productivity only so far. But when you have a mindset of being excited each and every morning, this provides you with a consistent motivation that keeps you going each and every day.

Grant Cardone

Grant Cardone is a real estate mogul, *New York Times* bestselling author, world-renowned sales expert, and top social media influencer. He owns and operates Grant Cardone TV Network, Cardone Capital, Cardone Acquisitions and Cardone University. Here are three brain hacks from him.

1. The best way to learn is by doing.

Grant Cardone was once interviewed in a Success Resources Australia podcast where he shared his experience of starting a new business.

Cardone says he started as an employee with an income of $100,000 per year and dropped to earning $30,000 per year with his new sales business, which he started at the age of 29.

In the beginning of his business, things were hard and he had to build his company by knocking on doors and making cold calls to hundreds and thousands of people. During that time, Cardone documented what was working and what was not working. He then started adjusting to his findings, which eventually made him successful. He concluded by saying the best way to learn is to do whatever you want and keep on doing it until it works.

The mentality of learning by doing is a mentality that resonates well with accelerated learning. This is because accelerated learning entails you learning the way you were designed to learn—and that is by you experiencing the lesson instead of just reading about the lesson. If you take an example like learning how to drive a car, you will notice that learning how to drive by actually driving is a much faster process than reading how to drive a car in a book or watching a YouTube video. So, to be successful in accelerated learning, you must adapt a mindset of learning by doing.

2. Connections are your most powerful commodity.

Grant Cordone normally says your most powerful commodity is your connections and not time or money. He says connections are your most valuable asset because when you build a good network, things start happening to you, including doors opening and opportunities presenting themselves to you.

You can use Cordone's mentality to succeed in accelerated learning.

How, you may ask? You can look at this in two ways:

- First, you can think of your five senses as being a good network, which you can connect and integrate in what you are learning to get better understanding and learn fast.

- Second, the network that you are supposed to connect with can be your peers, friends, workmates, or any other person or group that has the ability to add value to your learning.

This means you take multiple approaches to your learning—like using study groups, tutors, and even online tutorials that will help you accelerate your learning.

3. Set targets that are ten times the goals you dream of.

One important lesson from Grant Cardone is the lesson on how you should set your targets. He believes the best way to do this is by setting your targets higher than the goal you dream of.

For instance, if you want to go on a holiday in a three star hotel in France, he advocates you setting your target as: *"I want to book a business class ticket to France where I will spend my holiday in the best hotel in the country."*

That is an outrageous target.

Cardone says such a target pushes you to aim higher and do more to have a nice holiday, and even though you might not achieve that outrageous goal, you will end up in a position that is better than what you had anticipated at first.

For instance, instead of you going to a three star hotel, that extra push from the outrageous target will help you afford a four star one.

You can use this mentality to accelerate your learning by pushing yourself to do more when it comes to learning. For instance, instead of settling for the five-month period that your teacher told you it will take for you to learn German, you can set your deadline to two months. This will help you accelerate your learning, as you will put more effort in to understand the language.

With what we've learned so far, you should find it easy to intensify the process of you accelerating your learning.

Next, we will learn how to deal with setbacks you may experience while learning.

Chapter 10: Obstacles to Learning and Common Mistakes

Just like anything in life, learning has challenges. These challenges come in the form of obstacles that make you unable to learn optimally. Lucky for you, this chapter will highlight common mistakes and obstacles you may experience while learning and how you can deal with them.

1. Focusing too much on one thing.

Focusing too much on one thing is a huge obstacle that stands in the way of self-learning.

How?

Have you ever tried to learn one thing for the whole day without taking breaks to focus on something else? If you have, you know how fast your motivation toward learning gradually drops as the day goes by. You may start the day very motivated and passionate about that one thing you are learning but if you keep at it for too long, frustrations and boredom kick in. It may get to a point where you don't feel like continuing with the activity anymore.

The reason why this is the case, is because your brain naturally gets tired when you stick too much focus on one thing.

So how can you overcome this obstacle that has the potential to slow down or even ruin your plans of accelerating your learning?

The answer is that you need to learn how your brain works and then follow what comes naturally to it.

So how does your brain work?

Your brain naturally craves to learn different things within the day because that is how it works more efficiently.

Therefore, what you should do to avoid this obstacle is to spread what you are studying out into different learning tasks.

You can use either of two approaches:

- You can use different styles to learn one thing. For example, you can break down learning how to play a keyboard into theory lessons, practical lessons, study group lessons and tutorial lessons. Here, you can switch between the lessons throughout the day, which will help you not to tire and frustrate your brain.

- The second way is by you spreading out different subjects to learn during the day. For instance, learn to play a keyboard for two hours then move to learning math for one hour, chemistry for two hours and history for two hours.

2. Not paying attention to basics.

The worst thing you can ever do when trying to accelerate your learning is to not pay attention to the basics of what you are learning. It is one of the biggest obstacles to learning because it will not only lead to you failing to learn what you are supposed to, but it can also kill your interest in a specific method of learning or in a specific subject.

For example, if you look at the 80/20 rule, you will realize it is a very good strategy when it comes to helping you learn any skill fast. That said, it only works when you do basic groundwork of discovering the 20 percent of your input that drives 80 percent of your outcome. For instance, if you use the 80/20 rule to learn Spanish but you ignore the basic process of finding out which learning method helps you get a greater outcome when learning foreign languages, you will end up learning Spanish in a method that does not drive the 80 percent outcome of understanding you are looking for. Unfortunately, not paying attention to basics will make you not achieve your goal of learning Spanish at a fast rate, and it may also kill your desire to use the 80/20 rule; a really good strategy if used right.

To overcome this obstacle, you simply need to pay attention to the basics. The basics of a skill are the foundation of a skill and the part that makes the skill a success. So, always strive to master the basics of a skill first before you implement it.

3. Not believing in yourself.

The biggest obstacle to you accelerating your learning is YOU. What you tell yourself is usually what you think about yourself and what eventually happens to your life. For instance, if you tell yourself you can't speed-read, you will definitely not be able to speed-read.

Indeed, the obstacle to you learning is that small voice that whispers words of self-doubt to you like, "You are not good enough," "There is no way you can learn German in two months," and "You will never be able to name all the nine planets."

The solution to you not believing in yourself is to always be positive toward your abilities. Turn that small voice that is whispering negative words into a voice that whispers positive words. Tell yourself, "I am good enough" and "I can learn a new language in two months." Just tell yourself, "I can do it" and repeat that whenever you want to learn how to accelerate your learning.

You should also stop beating yourself up because you have faced a setback. It happens to the best of us and the right thing to do is to keep on moving. For instance, if you know how to ride a bicycle, you know that to learn it, you had to fall down a couple of times but that falling didn't stop you from continuing to learn how to ride the bicycle. That's how you should be; continue learning regardless of the setbacks.

4. Comparing yourself to professionals.

Comparing yourself to professionals is a major obstacle to learning. Why?

We all have this tendency of wanting to be as good as the best people who lead in the fields that we are interested in. It may seem like a good way to model the lives of successful people but what we don't understand is that those people took years to be where they are.

For instance, if you are an IT student and you compare yourself to Bill Gates, what will happen is you will end up feeling like your knowledge and abilities are nothing in the eyes of Bill Gates. What this will do is discourage you from learning, as it's very easy for you to be discouraged by the abilities of professionals.

To deal with this problem, you will need to learn about something that interests and excites you. Something that challenges you and takes all your focus. This is because when you do so, you won't be worried too much about what other people are doing in your line of interest; you will instead focus on you bettering yourself.

Let's say for example you love reading novels. It will be easy for you to learn how to speed read without you comparing yourself to the speed of Tim Ferriss because your joy will be in reading more books than you did before. Focus on being your best.

The bottom line here is; take advice from professionals but don't compare yourself with them.

5. Not celebrating your success.

We all feel bad and beat ourselves up when we make mistakes or when we fail; the only difference is the intensity with which we beat ourselves up!

If you look at your life, you will notice how easy it is for you to feel like a failure in something even though you have been making huge achievements.

Here is an example; remember that time in high school when it was time to receive your results? You could perform well in some subjects and badly in others but all you would go home thinking about is why and how you failed those few subjects.

The behavior of not celebrating your victories or looking at the bright side is one of the obstacles to learning. This is because when you are fast to feel bad about making a mistake and slow to feel good about your accomplishments, you decrease your motivation to do what you are doing, which makes it harder for you to achieve your goals.

For instance, if you are learning a new language and all you think week in week out is how you never hit your target, the chances of you quitting French become very high.

The solution here is for you to track your progress regularly to realize how far you have come. This enables you to recognize your achievements and celebrate them. Celebrating your accomplishments activates the reward circuits in your brain. The neurotransmitter dopamine is released when you celebrate something, which gives you the feel-good feeling that energizes and motivates you to achieve more. That feeling also encourages you to do what you did repeatedly so that you can trigger that good feeling again. So, if you want to be successful in fast learning a new language, celebrate your achievements.

6. Procrastination.

Have you ever been given a two-week deadline on a project at work or an assignment in school and you found yourself putting the assignment off until the last two days where you now had to do it in a hurry? That is called procrastination and it happens to the best of us.

Procrastination, which is ignoring unpleasant but important tasks to attend to easy, enjoyable and less important tasks, is the number one enemy to learning. This is because it is a powerful habit that can put a stop to even the best learning methods. The good news is that you can overcome this damaging habit of delaying important tasks. How?

By following these steps:

Step 1: Know when you are procrastinating.

You may be so used to ignoring important tasks in favor of less important tasks but for you to rectify that, you first must know when you do so. Here are a few signs that you can look out for to know you are procrastinating:

- You start a high priority task and you get an urge to do something else like making coffee or returning a missed call. At this point, you are about to procrastinate.

- Your day is filled with low priority tasks only.

- You have been ignoring an item on your to-do list for a long time now.

Step 2: Find the reason why you are procrastinating.

The second step is for you to think and find out why you are procrastinating.

- Is the task you are avoiding unpleasant or boring?
- Are you a perfectionist who fears not having the skills to perfectly execute the task you are ignoring?
- Do you have trouble deciding where to start with a particular task?

Step 3: Overcome your procrastination.

Once you find out why you procrastinate, you will need to come up with strategies that will overcome your reason for procrastinating.

For instance:

- If a task is unpleasant to you, you can establish the long-term benefits of accomplishing the tasks to overcome procrastination. For instance, if you are working at a delivery company and after a closer look at your situation you realize that the harder you work, the bigger your end-year bonus is, you will most definitely stop procrastinating and work hard in order to get a bigger bonus at the end of the year.

- The other way you can overcome procrastination is reviewing the consequences of you not doing that task. For instance, not working on your productivity may lead to you being laid off. That consequence will motivate you to focus on doing the task without procrastinating.

- If you are procrastinating because the projects you are doing are overwhelming, you can try breaking the task into small manageable tasks. Plan to deal with each task with your focus being to do the tasks rather than to finish the task.

- If you are disorganized, you can go ahead and start keeping a daily to-do list and follow it. This way, you won't leave any task you have behind.

- That said, changing your procrastination habit is possible but it will take time, so you need to give yourself time to make the shift.

Let's now focus on the mistakes you may be making that could be slowing down your learning process.

Common Mistakes and How to Fix Them

Here are the common mistakes you make in learning and how you can overcome them.

1. You are not interested in what you are learning.

No subject, topic or skill is boring to learn. All subjects are interesting. This is because every topic has a natural appeal; the deal is you finding an interesting way to learn about that topic. For instance, learning agriculture may be considered boring by many but what people don't know is that when you learn agriculture in a place where you can see how plants are grown and animals are kept, the subject becomes very interesting.

This shows you can be interested in the subjects that you think are boring if you stop using boring ways to learn them and instead use interesting ways to learn about them.

So how can you make everything that you learn interesting?

The key and the solution to making whatever subject you are learning interesting is for you to connect whatever you are learning with something that you care about.

For instance, in accelerated learning, the subject of memory retention may be uninteresting and boring to you because it not only makes you remember the important details that you need to remember but it also makes you remember words or sayings that represent that information. What you can do with it is you can turn the lesson into a game that makes thinking in this way some sort of treasure hunt. So, think of the process of you retaining information in your memory as a treasure hunt and the mnemonics techniques as your clues to finding the answers. This will automatically make memory retention an interesting subject for you.

So always look for connections that interest you when you are about to study a subject you seem uninterested in.

2. Memorizing instead of understanding.

As a student, many of the lessons you learn in school are lessons that are supposed to help you through life.

For instance, if you are studying to be a French interpreter, knowing the language will be the most important thing for you. Therefore, if you just memorize the language instead of understanding it, you will end up not knowing the language very well, which will make you miss out on the opportunity of being a French interpreter.

Here is another example: in accelerated learning, you are taught how to remember the order of operation in math using the acronym PEDMAS, which stands for Parentheses, Exponent, Division, Multiplication, Addition and Subtraction. Now memorizing this formula isn't as powerful as you understanding that this order of operation was set to make sure that every student got a similar answer when solving an equation with brackets, multiplication, subtraction and the rest. This is because there are many ways you can solve a question like that and almost each method has a different answer. When you understand that, you tend to approach the formulae with a deeper insight that makes you remember it for years or even for life.

3. Not doing enough practice.

Your learning process normally suffers when you don't practice what you have learned enough. You may think that re-reading a book or going through your notes is practicing but it is not and that's where you go wrong.

To solve this mistake, you need to practice properly and there are two ways of going about it.

First is by you performing a skill that you have just learned about. For instance, since we learned memory retention through chunking, that's what we will use in our example. The best practice that you can carry out to remember what you were taught is for you to frequently chunk long numbers that you come across like your friend's cell phone number or even your social security number, passport number et cetera.

Second, you can practice by self-testing yourself to see if you are recalling what you have learned. For instance, if you were in a chemistry class and you were taught how to make a mixture using acidic and basic liquids with the help of you involving multiple senses, you can self-test yourself after a day or so by challenging yourself to make the solution from scratch without referring to your book. If you remember, good for you—but if you don't, go back to your notes and check for the answer. This process of rechecking your notes helps you remember what you have learned even more.

4. Not choosing the right environment.

It is easier for you to create one big change that can enhance your learning than creating many small changes. The environment you are learning in is usually one of those big changes you can create to learn more and in a speedy manner with the same amount of determination and intelligence.

For instance, let's consider how to learn to be productive at work. One way you can do this is to take evening classes on productivity or read books on perfecting your productivity. That said, those options will never beat a method like you on taking a demanding project at work.

Why?

A demanding project at work will put you under pressure to perform better than you do in normal circumstances. This forces you to increase your productivity because the success of that project depends on it.

As you can see, the environment within which you learn really influences how well and fast you learn. Reading a book or taking a productivity class doesn't put you under pressure and that's why you become more productive in the second method that puts you under pressure.

So, if you want to learn how to speed-read, you have a better chance to learn faster if you join a reading competition rather than practicing fast reading on your own.

You are now almost completely equipped with all the knowledge that you need to start accelerating your learning. The only thing left now is for you to make a learning plan that will guide you through the process of accelerated learning. Let's now look at how to go about that.

Chapter 11: Bonus: The Accelerated Learning Plan Worksheet

There is a popular saying that goes something like this, "If you fail to plan, you are planning to fail." Planning is essential when it comes to you accomplishing your goal.

Planning will help you have an organized method of setting your goals. Apart from that, it also helps you to create a step-by-step pathway that you can use to reach your goals.

What is a learning plan?

A learning plan is simply a plan that sketches learning and the development measures to be taken within a specific timeframe. This plan is meant to assist you as a learner to achieve your learning goals and targets.

How Do You Create a Learning Plan?

Here are some steps you will need to follow to create a learning plan:

Step 1: Set goals.

The first step for you to create your learning plan is setting clear goals that you want to achieve. In your case, your goal is to accelerate your learning to be able to learn new skills fast, improve memory, develop laser-sharp focus, and increase your productivity through accelerating your learning.

Step 2: Decide the necessary steps to take.

The second step is to come up with the necessary steps that you should take to accelerate your learning. This guide has provided you with steps to follow to achieve goals; like how to speed-read, how to learn new things fast and much more. So, in this step, all you have to do is to lay those steps down on your learning worksheet.

Step 3: Create a timeline for your learning plan.

This step is simple; you need to create a timeline for your goals so that you can balance the activities that you will be doing to achieve those goals and the duration each activity will take.

As you know, learning takes a long time. So, you should divide that time into activities.

Step 4: Improve your learning plan.

The last step to creating a learning plan is for you to keep on improving it. No learning plan is absolutely perfect so for you to stay on top of your game, you need to keep on adjusting it.

Here is a sample learning plan worksheet that you can follow.

Accelerated Learning Plan Worksheet		
Goals	*Strategies*	*Timeline*
1. *I want to learn new skills fast.*	Learn new skills fast by: • Deconstructing a skill into small pieces. • Implementing the 80/20 rule. • Using the Pomodoro technique. • Using the distributed practice method. See what works for you and stick with it.	10 days
2. *I want to improve my memory retention.*	• Use mnemonics techniques to improve the memory.	8 days
3. *I want to develop a laser sharp focus.*	Use the following strategies to improve your focus: • Pre-commit yourself to a task. • Meditate.	1 week

		• Create a not-to-do list. • Decide what is worth your attention. • Concentrate on one thing at a time. • Re-engineer information to make it interesting. • Take short breaks. • Eliminate distractions.	
4.	*I want to increase my productivity.*	• Implement the productivity lesson learnt from Elon Musk.	10 days
5.	*I want to improve my reading speed.*	• Apply Tim Ferriss speed-reading techniques.	10 days
6.	*I want to master my intention and success mindset.*	• Make a ritual. • Write down your intention. • Make yourself aware of your intentions. • Celebrate your achievements. • Start slowly and be patient.	5 days

Conclusion

We have come to the end of *Accelerated Learning: Discover How High Performers Learn New Skills Fast, Improve Memory, Develop Laser-Sharp Focus, and Increase Their Productivity Using Techniques Such as Speed Reading.*

Being a high performer is not restricted to a specific group of people. We can all be high performers who go on to become very successful, and you now know the tricks and techniques to learn new skills fast, improve memory, develop laser-sharp focus and increase your productivity. All you have to do is follow the advice from this audiobook and believe that you will achieve what you intend to achieve, plus so much more!

If you found the audiobook valuable, can you recommend it to others?

Click here to leave a review for this book on Amazon!

Thank you and good luck in your learning journey.

Check out another book by Gordon Cohen

www.ingramcontent.com/pod-product-compliance
Lightning Source LLC
LaVergne TN
LVHW041642060526
838200LV00040B/1684